MIKE MIGNOLA'S

™

WEIRD TALES
Volume Two

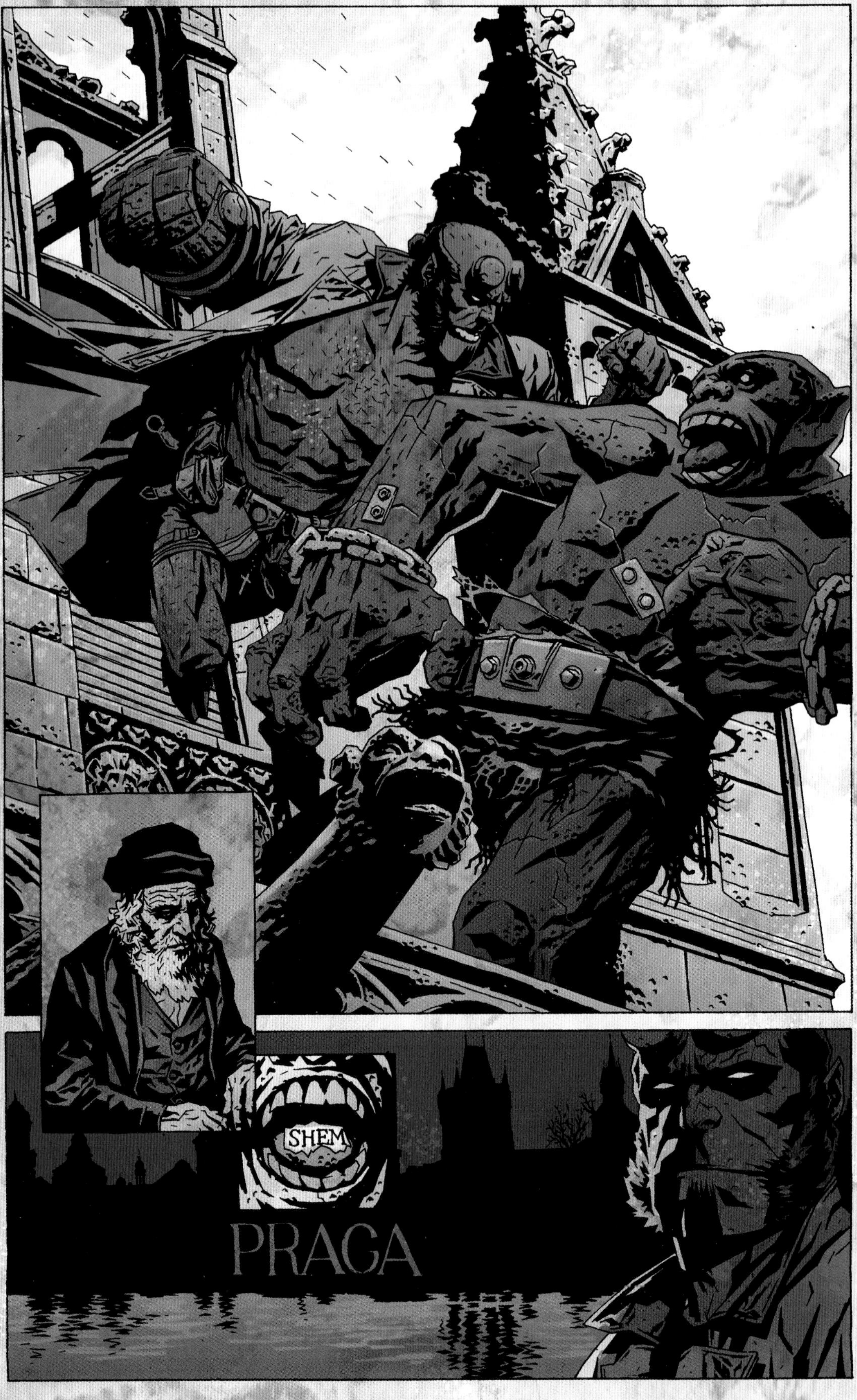
SHEM
PRAGA

MIKE MIGNOLA'S

WEIRD TALES
Volume Two

KIA ASAMIYA, LEE BERMEJO, HADEN BLACKMAN

JOHN CASSADAY, FRANK CHO, GENE COLAN, EVAN DORKIN

TOMMY LEE EDWARDS, TOM FASSBENDER, GARY FIELDS

MICHAEL WM. KALUTA, RON MARZ, SCOTT MORSE

PHIL NOTO, JIM PASCOE, DOUG PETRIE, WILL PFEIFER

STEVE PURCELL, P. CRAIG RUSSELL, JIM STARLIN, DAVE STEVENS

CAMERON STEWART, BEN TEMPLESMITH, CRAIG THOMPSON

JILL THOMPSON, KEV WALKER, SIMEON WILKINS

J.H. WILLAMS III & AKIRA YOSHIDA

✠

Cover art by MIKE MIGNOLA

Cover colors by DAVE STEWART

Edited by SCOTT ALLIE *with* MATT DRYER

Collection designed by RICHARD E. JONES

Published by MIKE RICHARDSON

DARK HORSE BOOKS™

MIKE RICHARDSON ✠ *publisher*

NEIL HANKERSON ✠ *executive vice president*

TOM WEDDLE ✠ *chief financial officer*

RANDY STRADLEY ✠ *vice president of publishing*

CHRIS WARNER ✠ *senior books editor*

MICHAEL MARTENS ✠ *vice president of business development*

ANITA NELSON ✠ *vice president of marketing, sales, & licensing*

DAVID SCROGGY ✠ *vice president of product development*

DALE LAFOUNTAIN ✠ *vice president of information technology*

DARLENE VOGEL ✠ *director of purchasing*

KEN LIZZI ✠ *general counsel*

LIA RIBACCHI ✠ *art director*

Published by Dark Horse Books
a division of Dark Horse Comics, Inc.
10956 SE Main Street
Milwaukie, OR 97222
www.darkhorse.com

First edition: October 2004
ISBN: 1-56971-953-5

This volume collects issues five through eight and the "Lobster Johnson" strips serialized in issues one through eight of the Dark Horse comic-book series, *Hellboy: Weird Tales.*

1 3 5 7 9 10 8 6 4 2

Printed in China

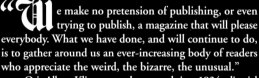

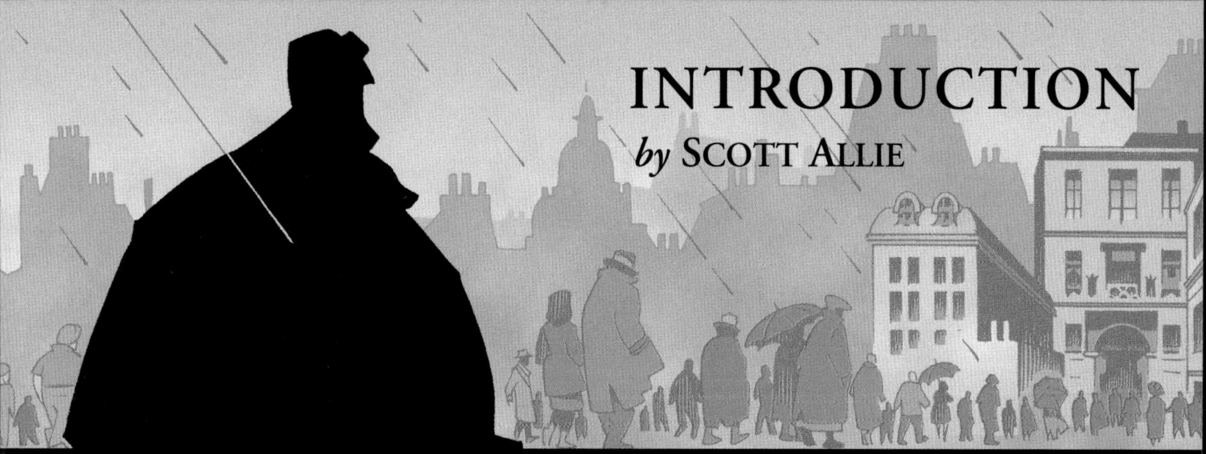

INTRODUCTION
by Scott Allie

"We make no pretension of publishing, or even trying to publish, a magazine that will please everybody. What we have done, and will continue to do, is to gather around us an ever-increasing body of readers who appreciate the weird, the bizarre, the unusual."

Otis Albert Kline wrote those words in a 1924 editorial in the pulp magazine *Weird Tales.* The magazine, which debuted in March of 1923, spent its first couple years struggling to stay alive, while publishing a unique brand of what Kline would call "highly imaginative stories," as though that were a specific genre. The magazine's first star, the first of many legends born from *Weird Tales*, was H.P. Lovecraft, who casts a shadow across all fantasy and horror fiction since, and whose stories exemplify the aesthetic and aspirations of the magazine. However, the pulp was plagued by financial disasters as it tried to shape an identity and to find its readership. In an attempt to solidify both, co-founders Jacob Clark Henneberger and J.M. Lassinger made a generous financial offer asking Lovecraft to leave Rhode Island for Chicago in order to edit the magazine. Lovecraft had just been married (and of course that didn't work out at all) and didn't want to relocate his bride to Chicago.

Instead Farnsworth Wright took over, becoming one of the most important editors in the history of macabre fiction. His first issue went on sale in November 1924. Wright brought in established writers like Kline and Seabury Quinn, but his more important contribution to the success of *Weird Tales* was in the form of his many discoveries, including Clark Ashton Smith, E. Hoffman Price, and Robert E. Howard, the creator of Conan. Wright paid top dollar for new stories—a penny a word, more for high-profile writers—keeping his writers well fed as America headed into the Depression. In 1930 the economy caught up with the magazine when the bank handling their business failed, and publication had to briefly go bimonthly—however, Wright continued paying as well as before. *Weird Tales* stayed strong through most of the Depression, until, in 1938 the magazine was sold and relocated to Manhattan. Wright stayed with it, but under new management, *Weird Tales* alienated readers and writers alike by cutting paper quality, cutting rates for writers and artists, and cutting page count—they also cut the cover price, but this didn't help. After two years in New York, Wright left the magazine, and *Weird Tales* went back to its bimonthly schedule.

The magazine's golden era was over, but it continued to introduce great writers, including Robert Bloch, Fritz Leiber, Ray Bradbury, and Manly Wade Wellman, some of the best horror and fantasy writers of the twentieth century. Over the next ten years, however, the magazine lost its direction, and in the early 1950s it was running more reprints than new stories. The magazine changed shape and size in an attempt to find a new home on the racks, until it ceased publication in March of 1954.

Fifty years after *Weird Tales* drifted into the void, it remains the most fondly remembered, and most immortalized of the pulps—reprint collections bearing the *Weird Tales* title continue to appear, and the magazine itself has resurfaced in many forms over the years, without ever quite recapturing the magic of Farnsworth Wright's initial run. Even if the magazine had only given us Lovecraft and Howard, its influence on horror and fantasy literature would be unparalleled. But all of the writers which it pushed into the pre-Hollywood American mainstream bore forward a literary tradition begun in the oldest stories of Western civilization, carried on by Homer and Shakespeare, Dante and Milton, Jules Verne and Charles Dickens. That tradition had been given a distinctive American voice by Nathaniel Hawthorne and Edgar Allan Poe, and it was Farnsworth Wright and the writers of *Weird Tales*—as well as artists like Hannes Bok, Lee Brown Coye, and Virgil Finlay—who gave it a new face in the early twentieth century. The best modern writers, from Stephen King to Joyce Carol Oates, are quick to acknowledge *Weird Tales*. As comics took their place as formal successor to the pulps, Bill Gaines and Al Feldstein at EC Comics in the 1950s and Roy Thomas and Len Wein and others in the 1970s drew inspiration from the greatest of the pulps. It was those comics that led Mike Mignola back up the ladder, tracing the origins and influences of their work back to *Weird Tales*. A voracious reader since his teenage years, Mignola soaked up as much of the original material as he could—demons and death rays and Nazis and things from beyond, things from the sea, lost civilizations, and noble brutes—until he could turn it back to the world in the form of Hellboy.

The word *weird* has lost some of its meaning in common American parlance, coming to signify nothing more than *unusual*, but its classic definition is easy to pinpoint for those of us who understand what Lovecraft, Wellman, and Leiber were up to in the pages *Weird Tales*.

Mike and I would like to thank everyone who worked on this book, to the authors who inspired us in the first place, and to Victor Dricks and Weird Tales Ltd. for allowing us to pay tribute in this unique way.

CONTENTS

PRAGUE...page 2
Art LEE BERMEJO ✠ *Colors* DAVE STEWART

MY VACATION IN HELL...page 7
Story and Art CRAIG THOMPSON

A LOVE STORY...page 15
Story TOMMY LEE EDWARDS ✠ *Art* TOMMY LEE EDWARDS
with DON CAMERON ✠ *Letters* JOHN WORKMAN

SHATTERED...page 23
Story RON MARZ ✠ *Art* JIM STARLIN
Colors DAVE STEWART ✠ *Letters* MICHELLE MADSEN

FRIDAY...page 31
Story DOUG PETRIE ✠ *Art* GENE COLAN
Colors DAVE STEWART ✠ *Letters* MICHAEL HEISLER

COMMAND PERFORMANCE...page 37
Story WILL PFEIFER ✠ *Art* P. CRAIG RUSSELL
Colors LOVERN KINDZIERSKI ✠ *Letters* GALEN SHOWMAN

LOVE IS SCARIER THAN DEATH...page 45
Story J.H. WILLAMS III and HADEN BLACKMAN
Art J.H. WILLAMS III ✠ *Letters* TODD KLEIN

THEATER OF THE DEAD...page 53
Story JIM PASCOE and TOM FASSBENDER ✠ *Art* SIMEON WILKINS
Colors DAVID SELF ✠ *Letters* ANNIE PARKHOUSE

TOY SOLDIER ...page 61
Story AKIRA YOSHIDA and KIA ASAMIYA ✠ *Art* KIA ASAMIYA
Colors DAVE STEWART ✠ *Letters* CLEM ROBBINS

PROFFESSIONAL HELP...page 71
Story and Art EVAN DORKIN ✠ *Colors* SARAH DYER

FIFTEEN MINUTES...page 81
Story and Art JILL THOMPSON

LONG DISTANCE CALLER...page 89
Story and Art KEV WALKER ✠ *Letters* MICHAEL HEISLER

COOL YOUR HEAD ...page 99
Story and Art SCOTT MORSE

LOBSTER JOHNSON...page 118
Story and Art JOHN CASSADAY ✠ *Colors* DAN JACKSON and NICK DERINGTON
Letters DAN JACKSON and JASON HVAM

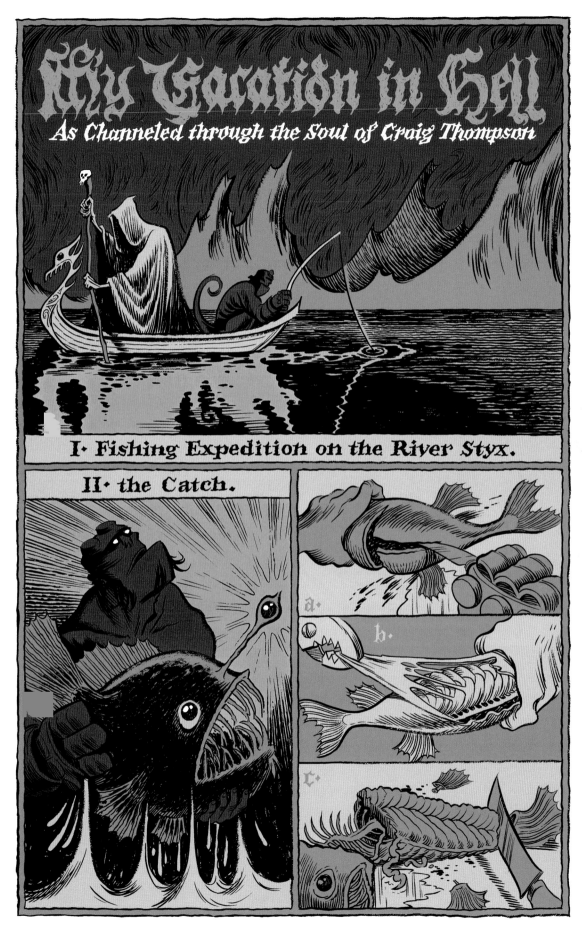

My Vacation in Hell

As Channeled through the Soul of Craig Thompson

I· Fishing Expedition on the River Styx.

II· the Catch.

a·

b·

c·

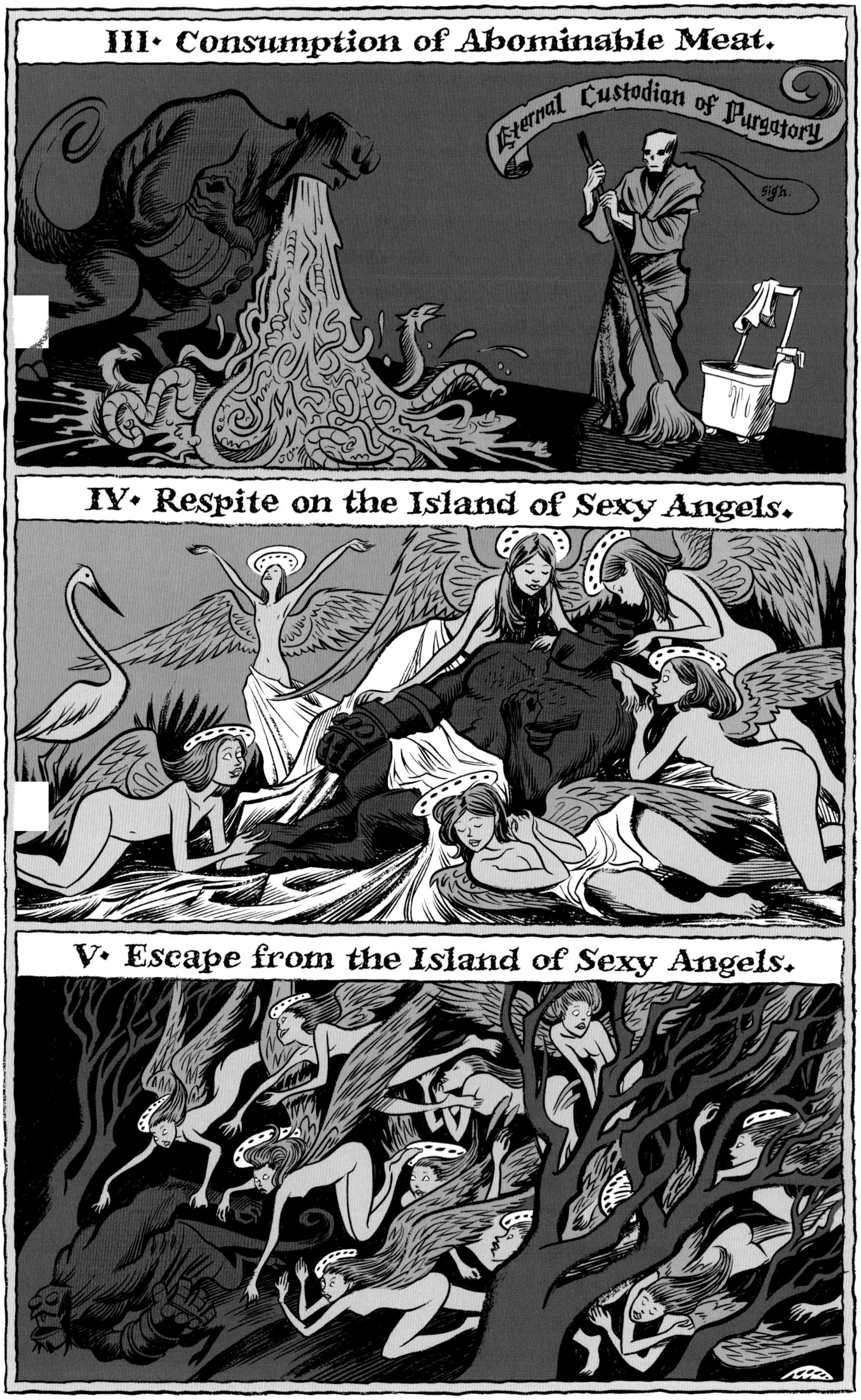
III· Consumption of Abominable Meat.
Eternal Custodian of Purgatory
sigh.
IV· Respite on the Island of Sexy Angels.
V· Escape from the Island of Sexy Angels.

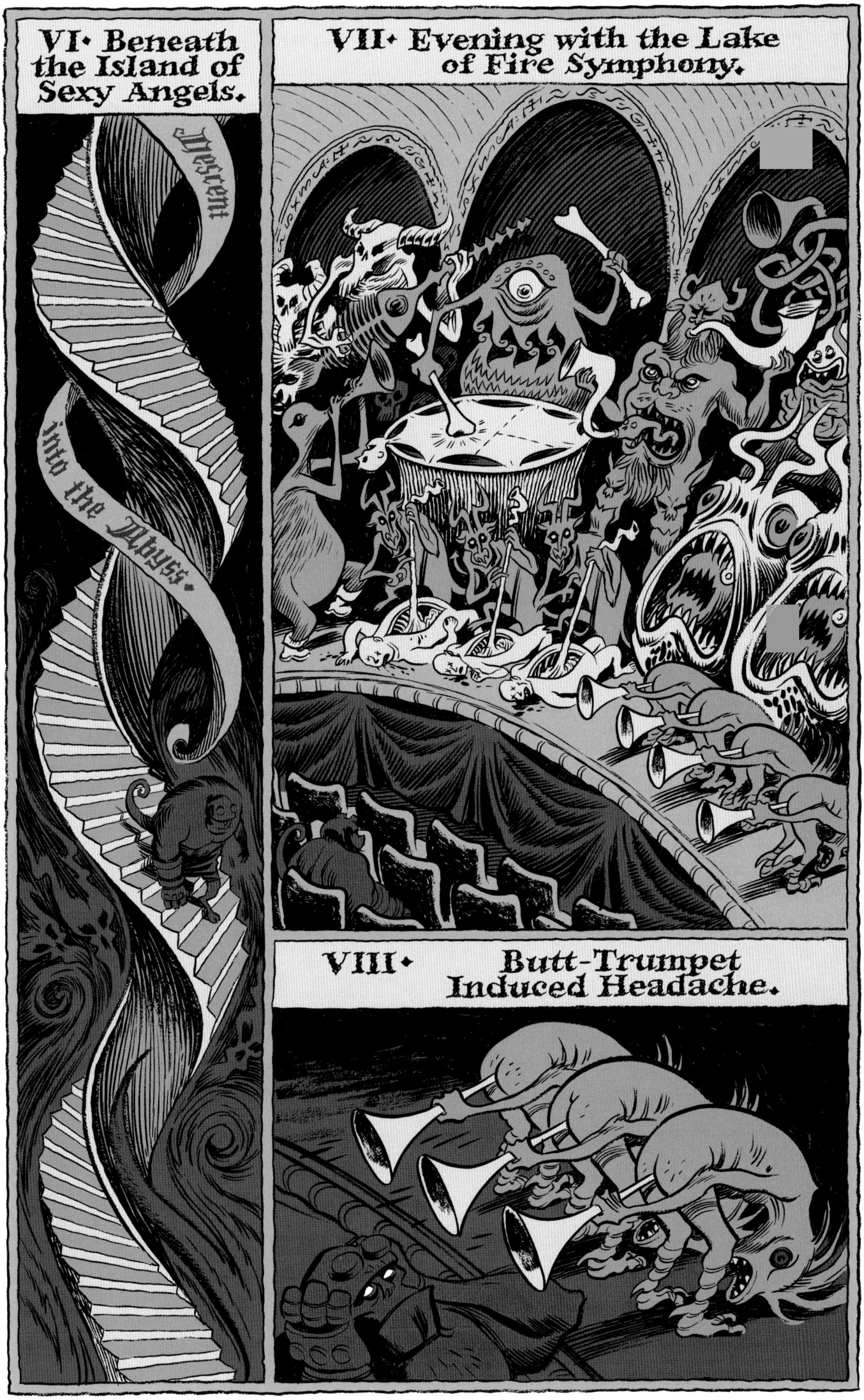
VI• Beneath the Island of Sexy Angels.
Descent into the Abyss•
VII• Evening with the Lake of Fire Symphony.
VIII• Butt-Trumpet Induced Headache.

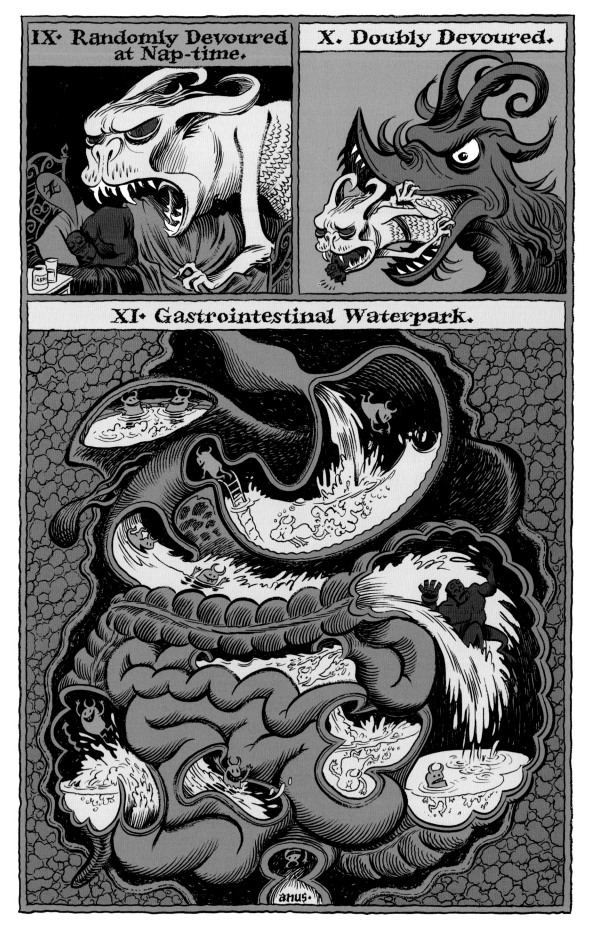

IX· Randomly Devoured at Nap-time.

X. Doubly Devoured.

XI· Gastrointestinal Waterpark.

anus·

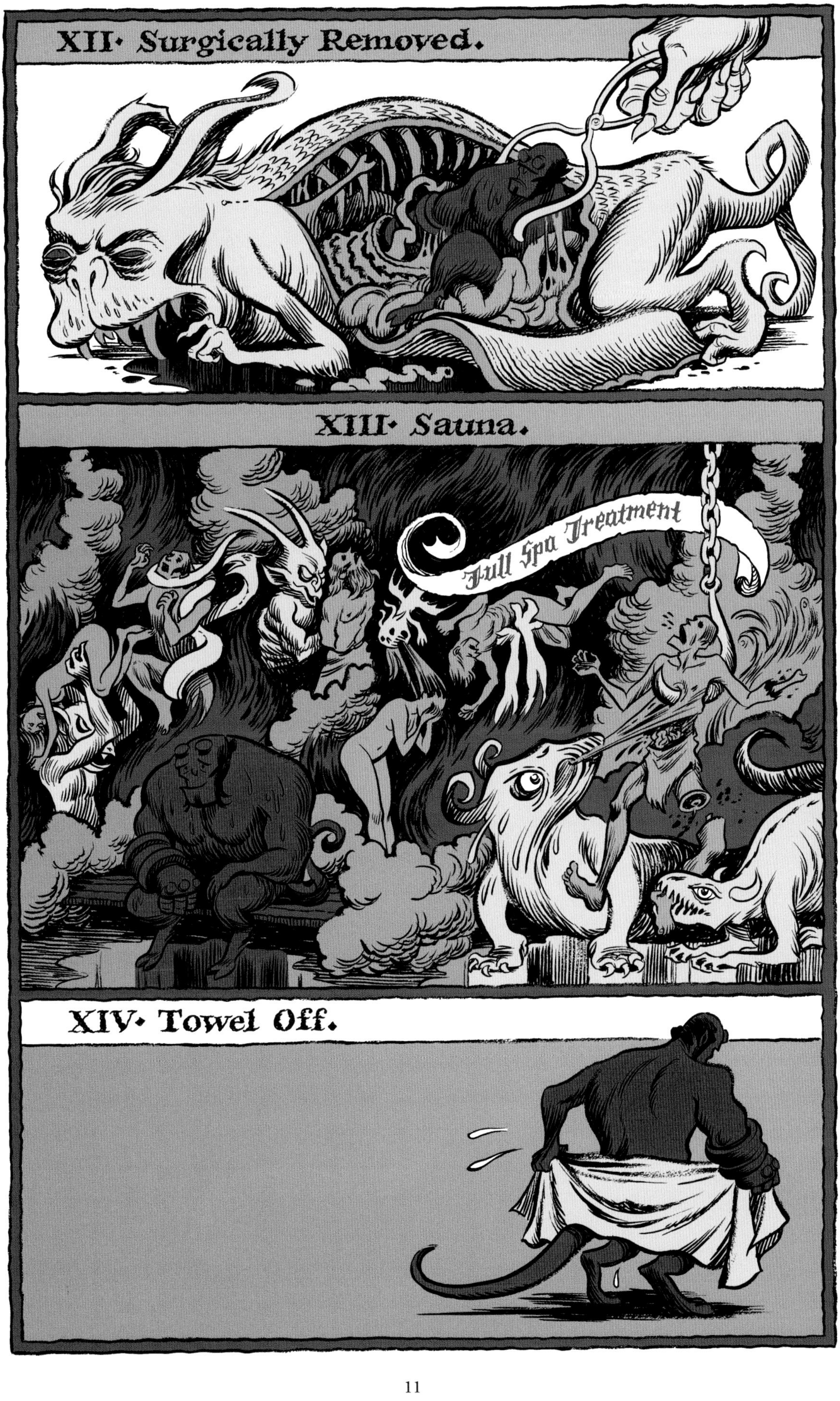
XII· Surgically Removed.
XIII· Sauna.
Full Spa Treatment
XIV· Towel Off.

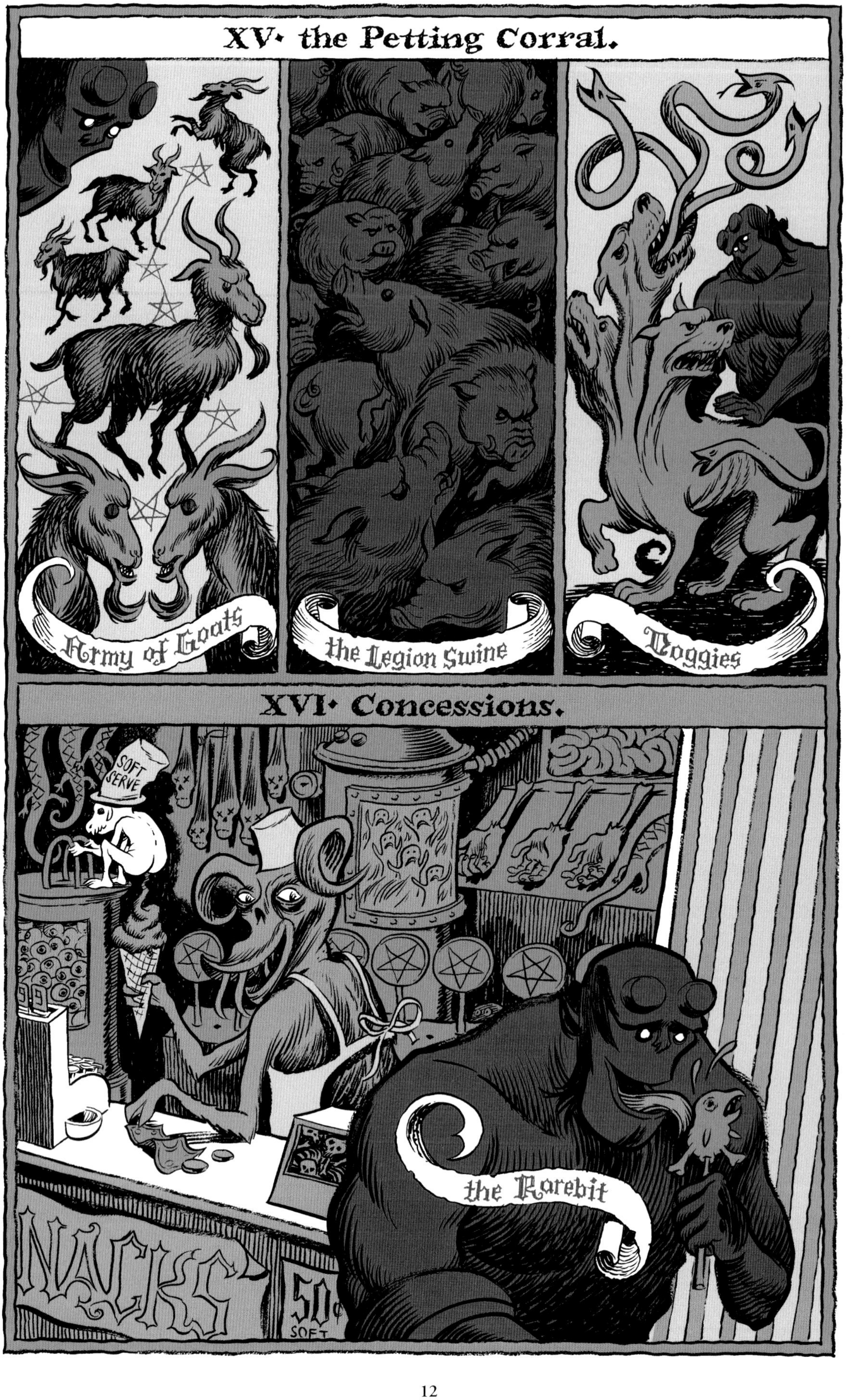
XV· the Petting Corral.
Army of Goats
the Legion Swine
Doggies
XVI· Concessions.
SOFT SERVE
the Rarebit
NACKS
50¢
SOFT

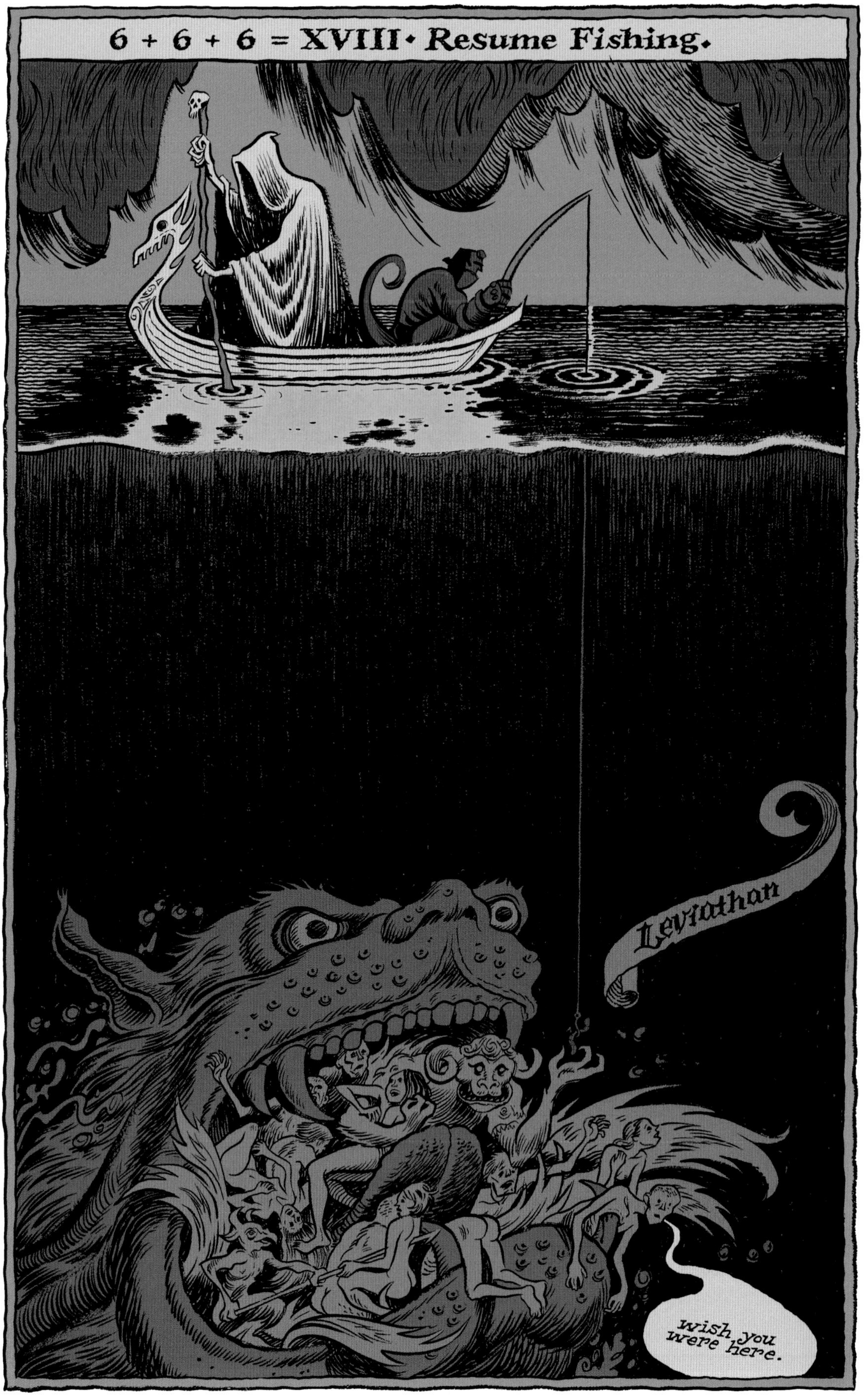
6 + 6 + 6 = XVIII • Resume Fishing.
Leviathan
wish you were here.

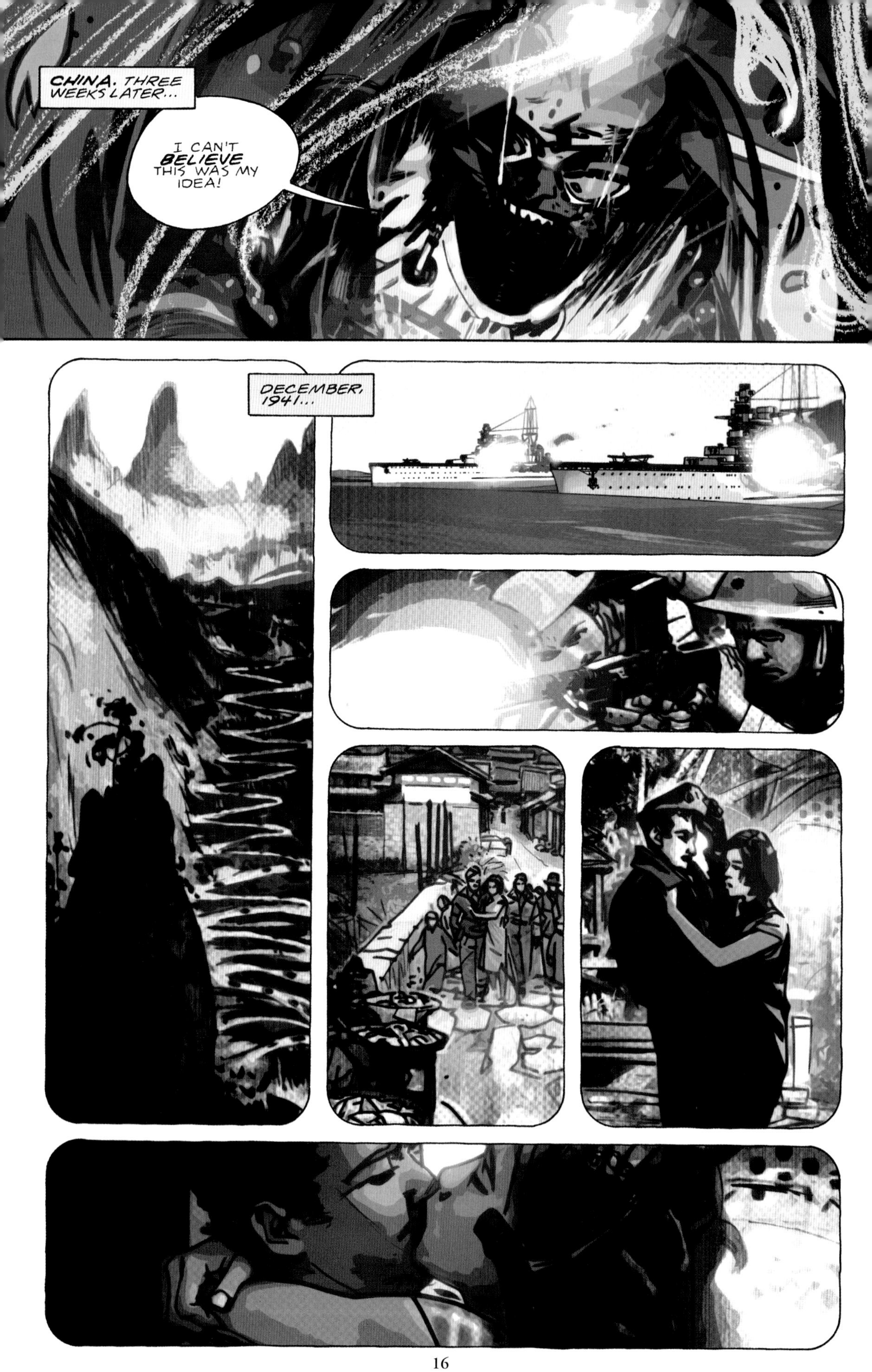
CHINA. THREE WEEKS LATER...
I CAN'T BELIEVE THIS WAS MY IDEA!
DECEMBER, 1941...

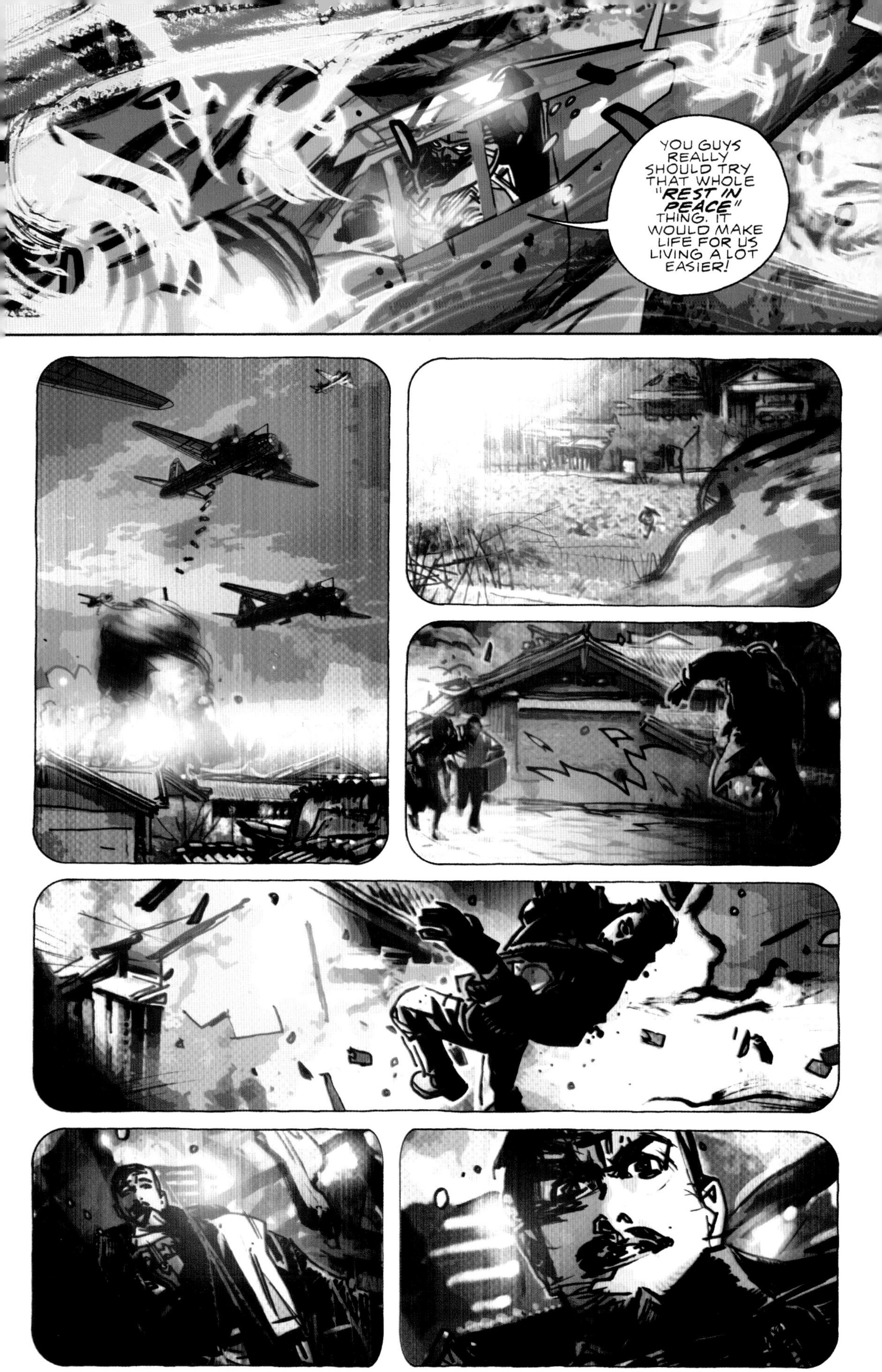
YOU GUYS REALLY SHOULD TRY THAT WHOLE "REST IN PEACE" THING. IT WOULD MAKE LIFE FOR US LIVING A LOT EASIER!

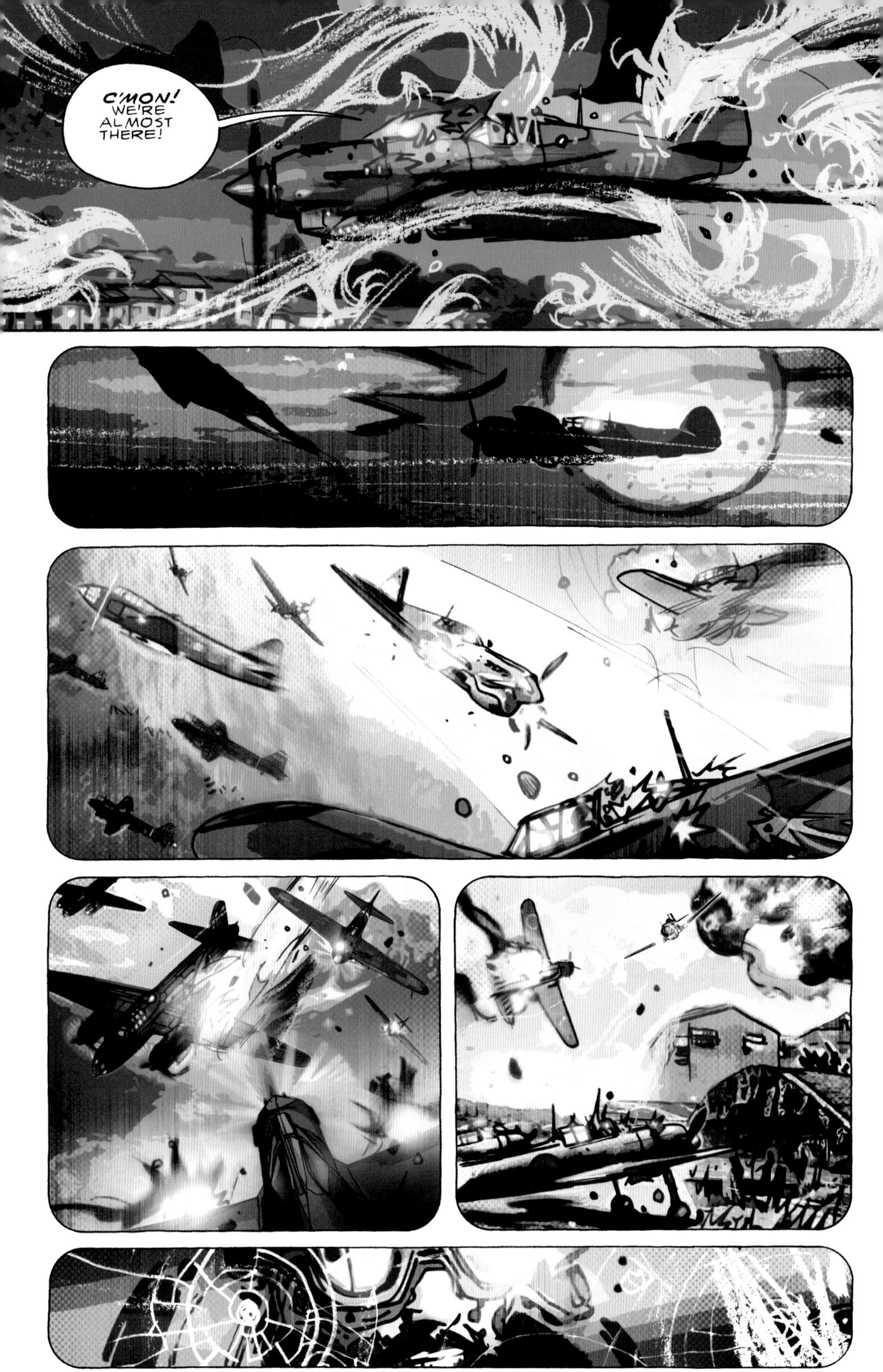
C'MON! WE'RE ALMOST THERE!

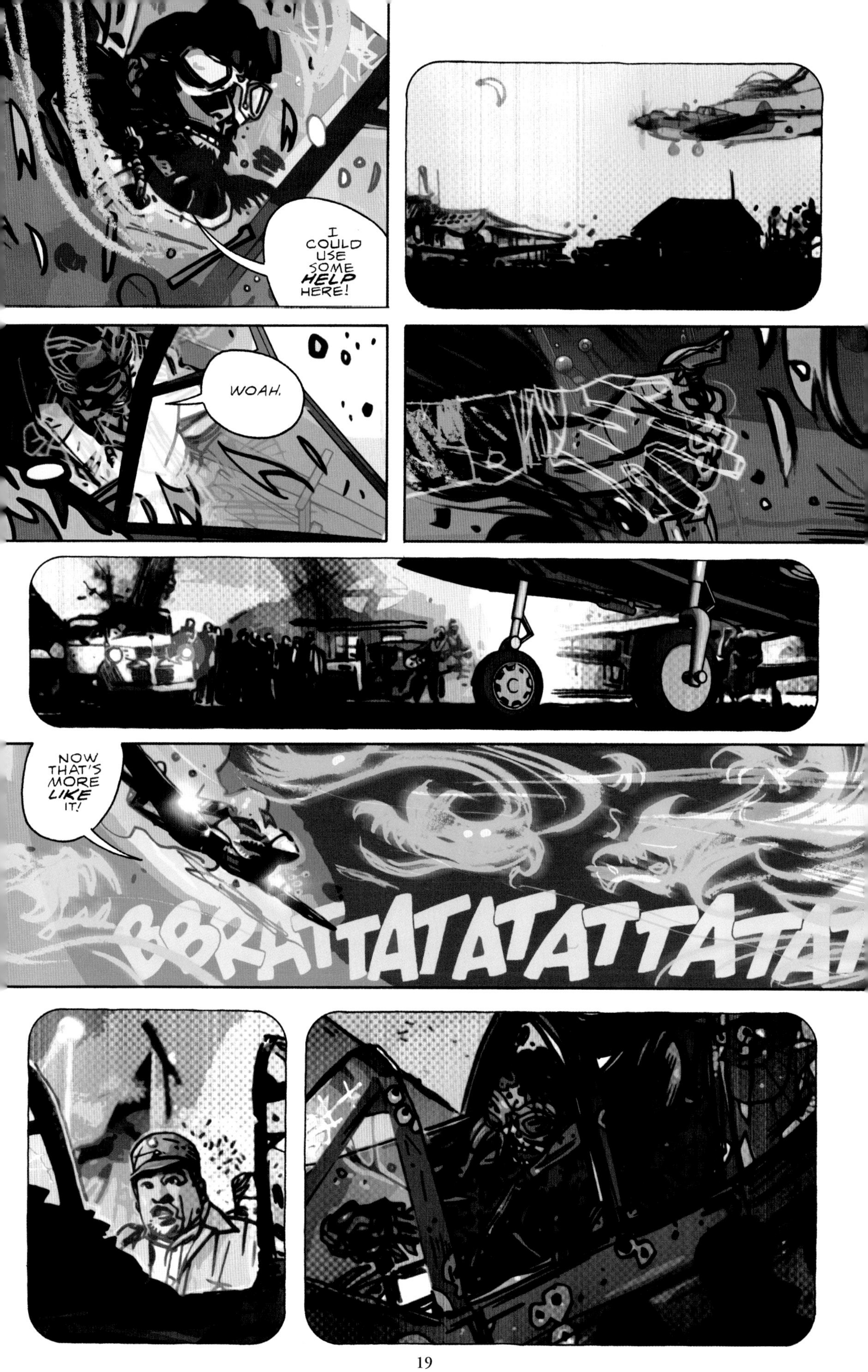
I COULD USE SOME HELP HERE!
WOAH.
NOW THAT'S MORE LIKE IT!
BBRATTATATATTATAT

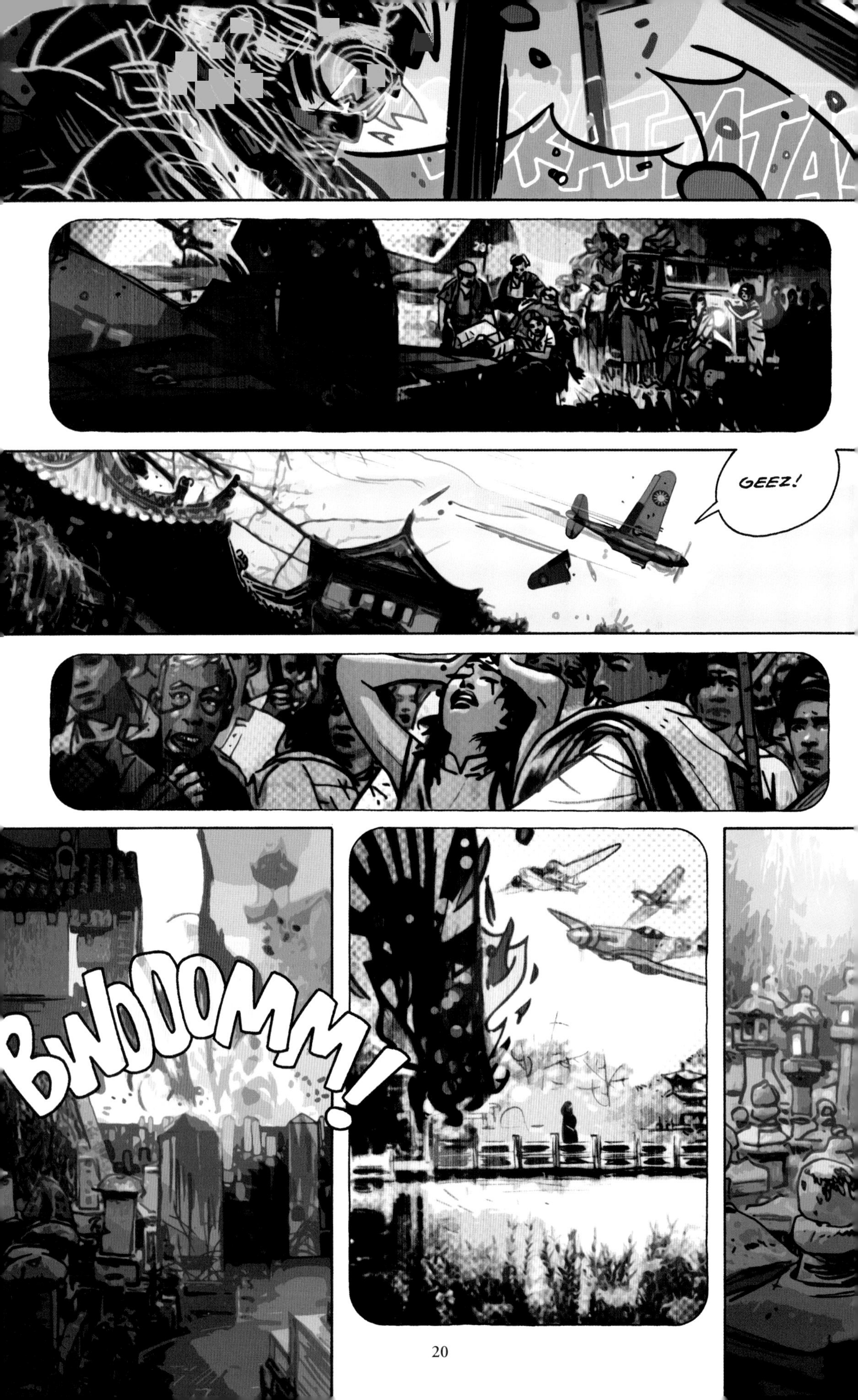
GEEZ!
BWOOOMM!

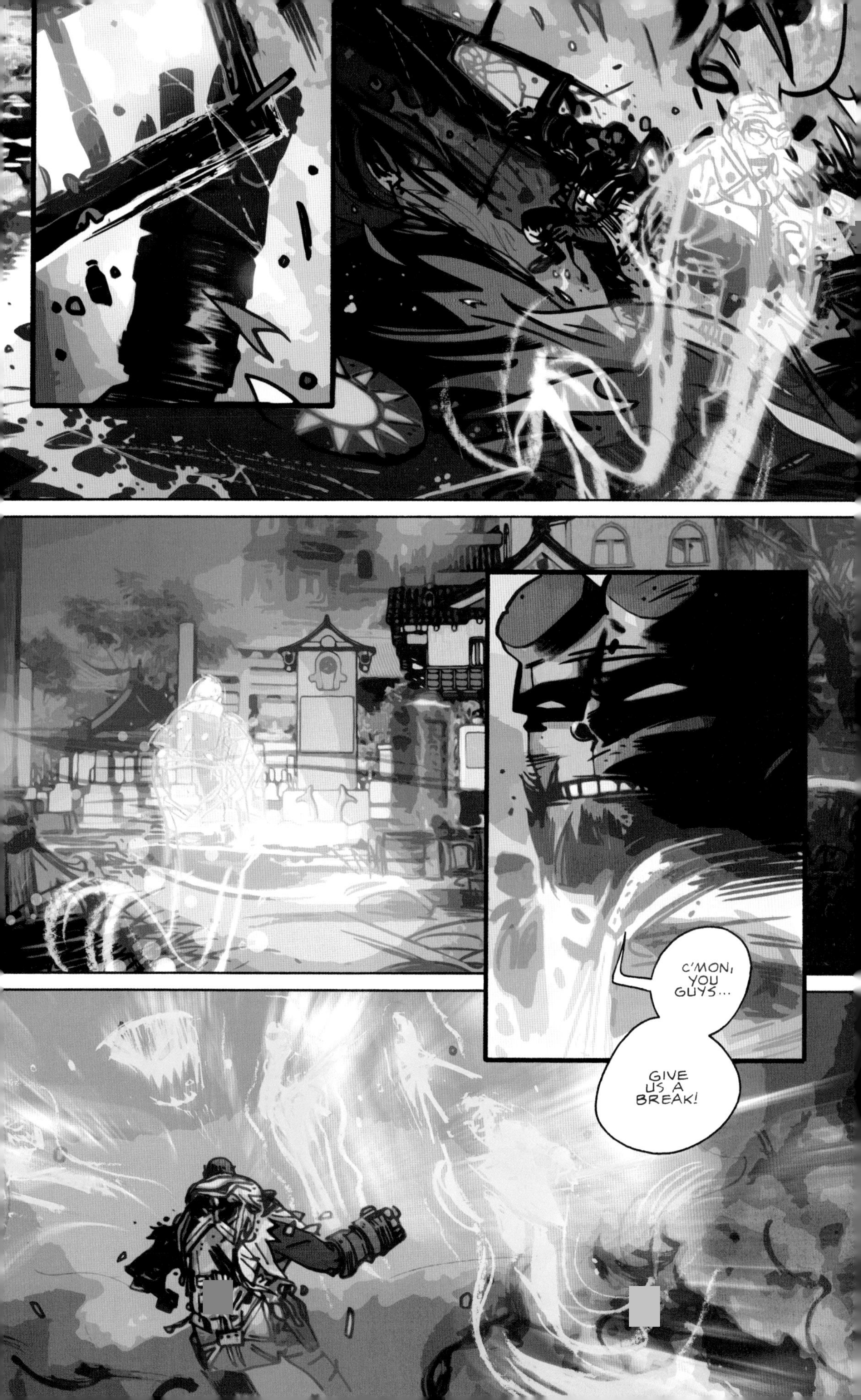
C'MON, YOU GUYS...
GIVE US A BREAK!

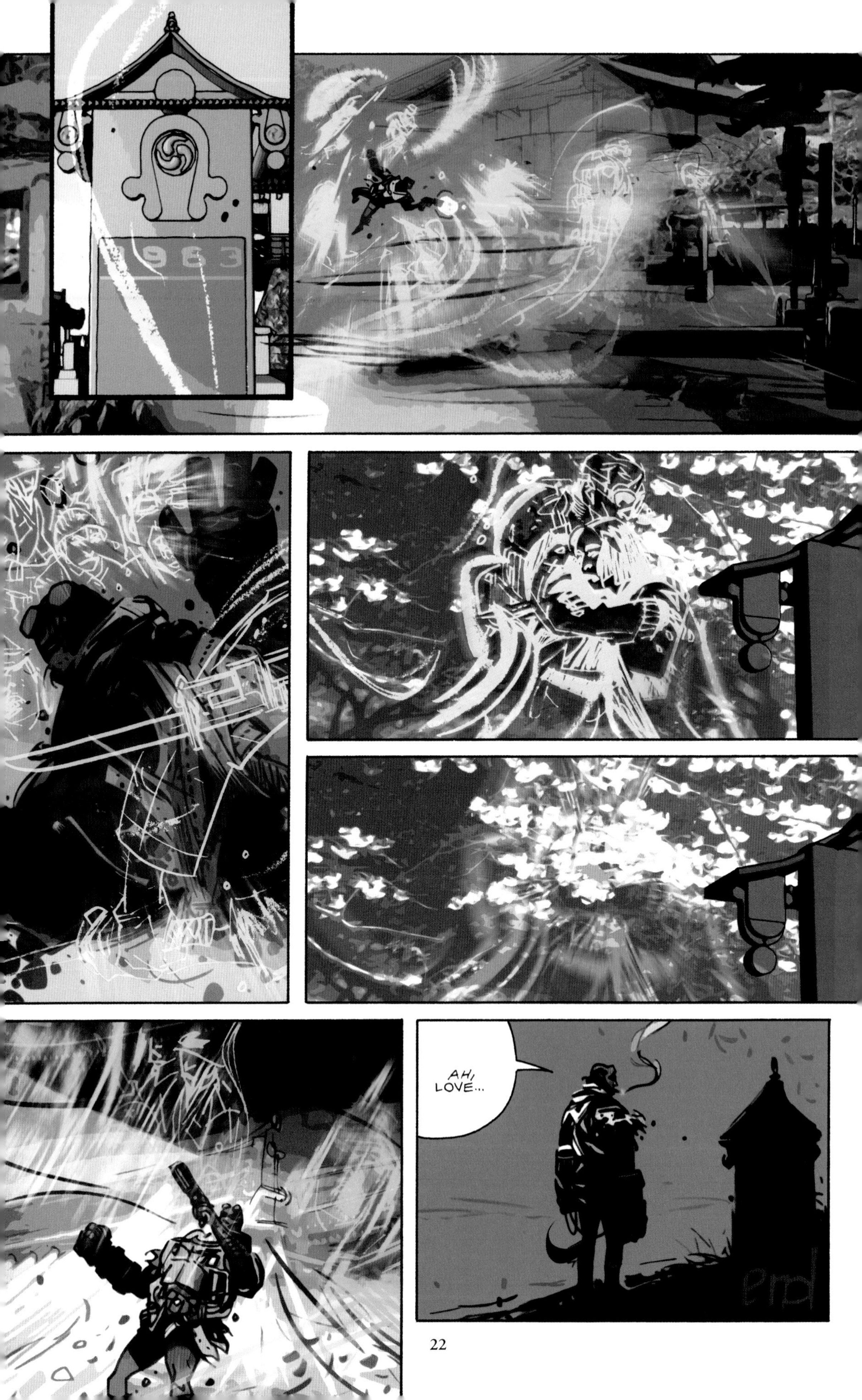
AH, LOVE...

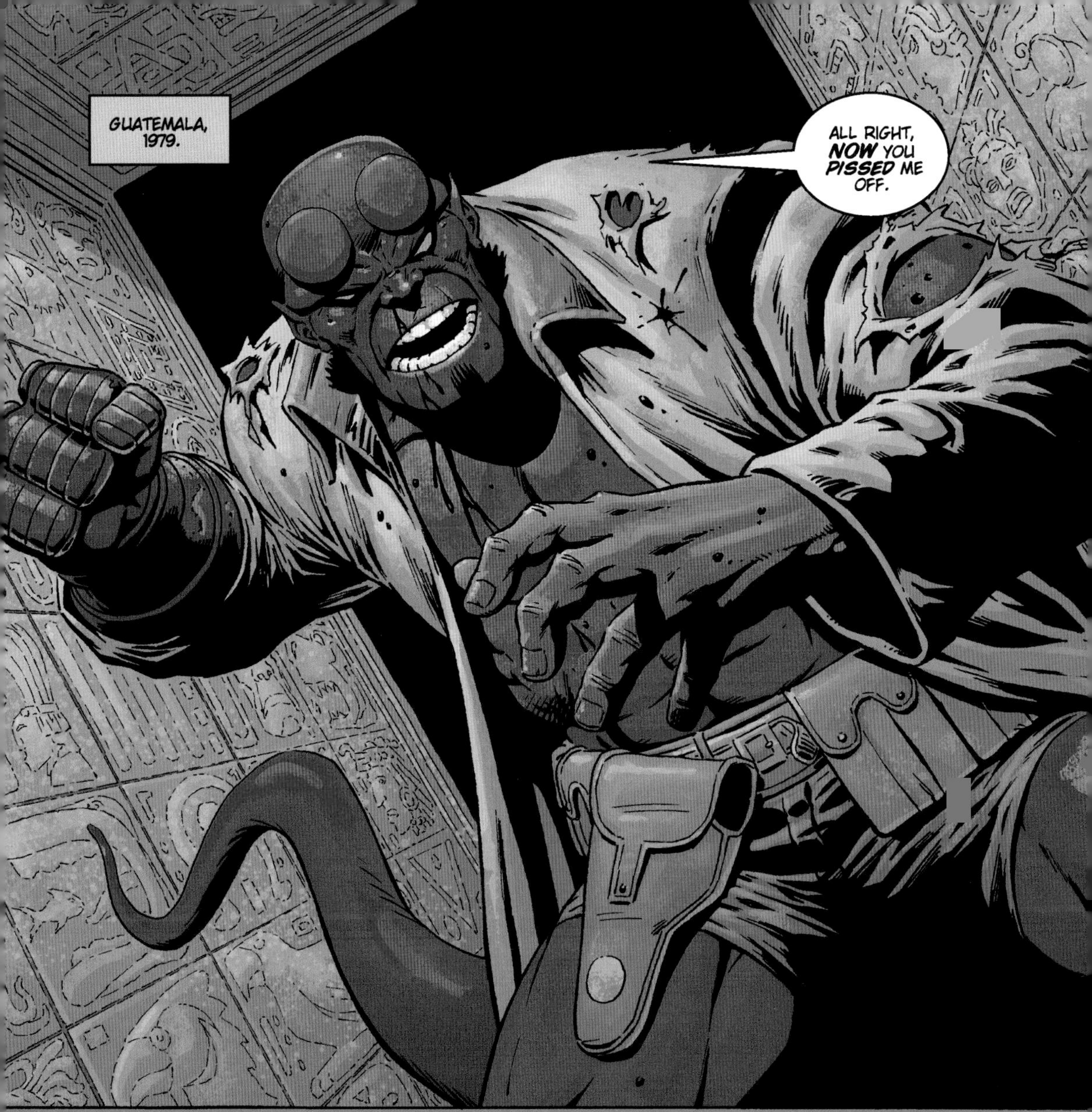
GUATEMALA, 1979.
ALL RIGHT, NOW YOU PISSED ME OFF.

SHATTERED

MARZ STARLIN STEWART MADSEN

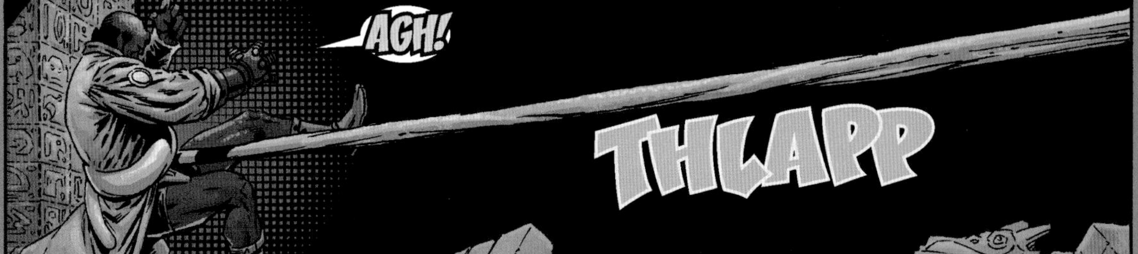
AGH!
THLAPP

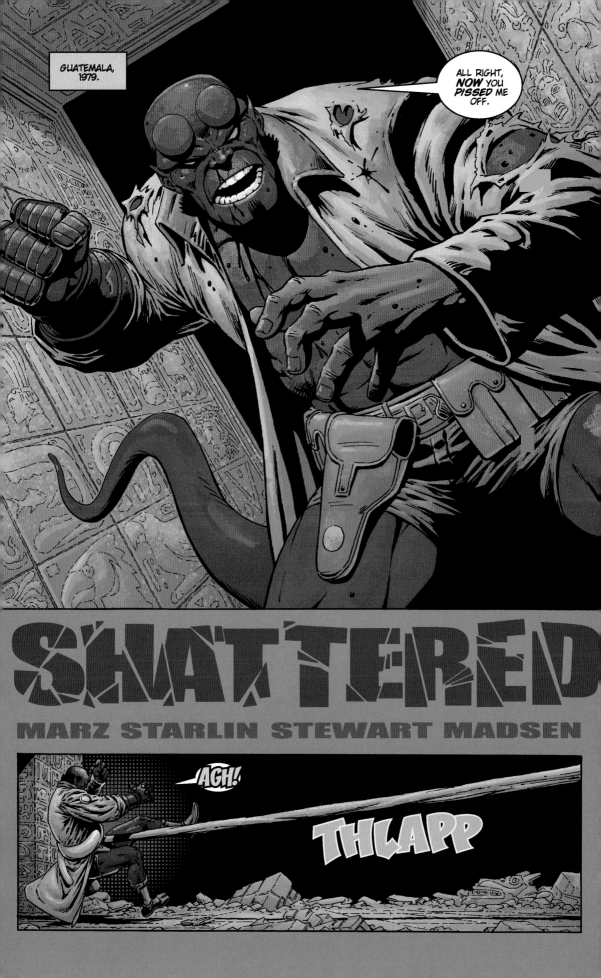

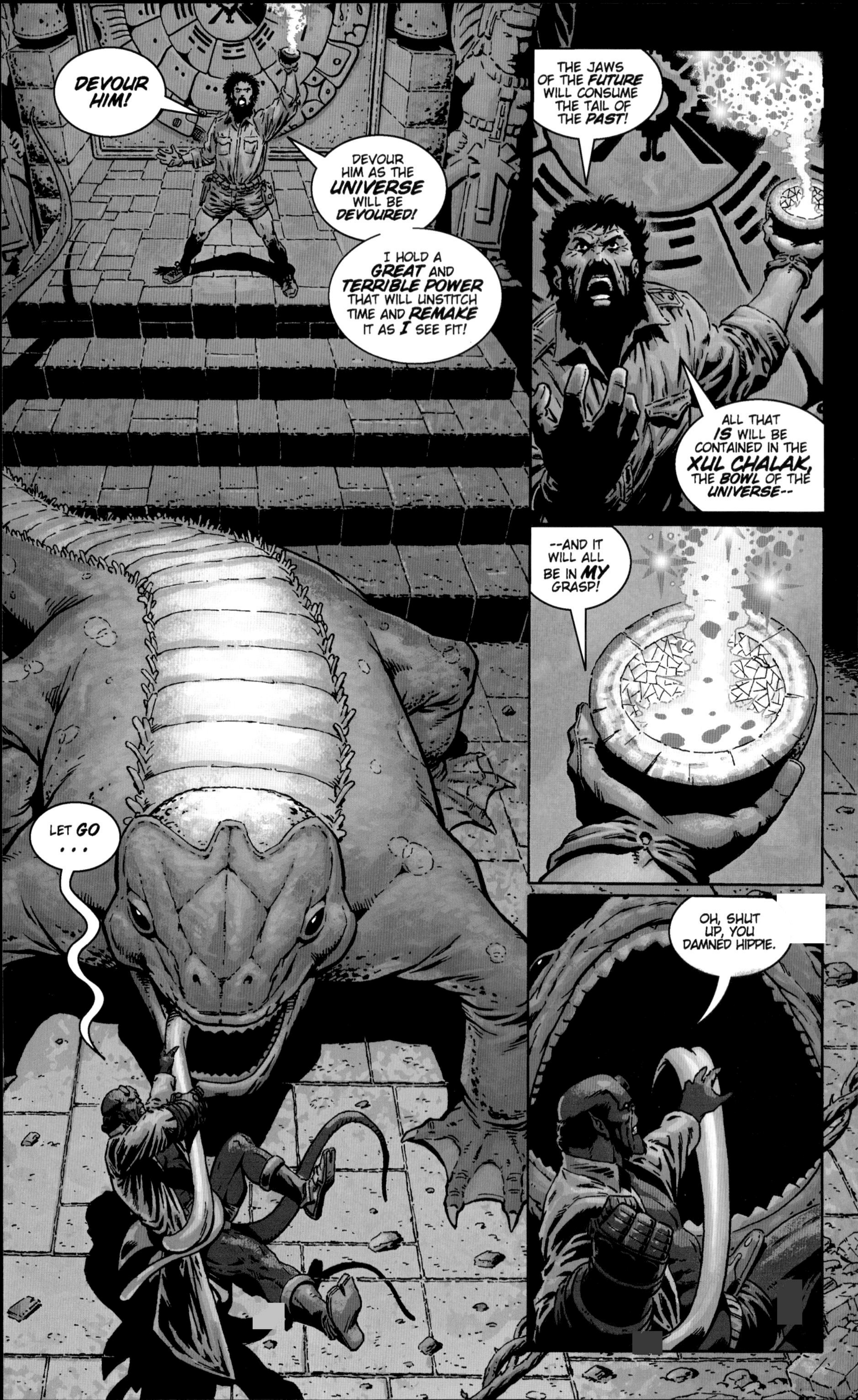
DEVOUR HIM!
DEVOUR HIM AS THE UNIVERSE WILL BE DEVOURED!
I HOLD A GREAT AND TERRIBLE POWER THAT WILL UNSTITCH TIME AND REMAKE IT AS I SEE FIT!
THE JAWS OF THE FUTURE WILL CONSUME THE TAIL OF THE PAST!
ALL THAT IS WILL BE CONTAINED IN THE XUL CHALAK, THE BOWL OF THE UNIVERSE--
--AND IT WILL ALL BE IN MY GRASP!
LET GO . . .
OH, SHUT UP, YOU DAMNED HIPPIE.

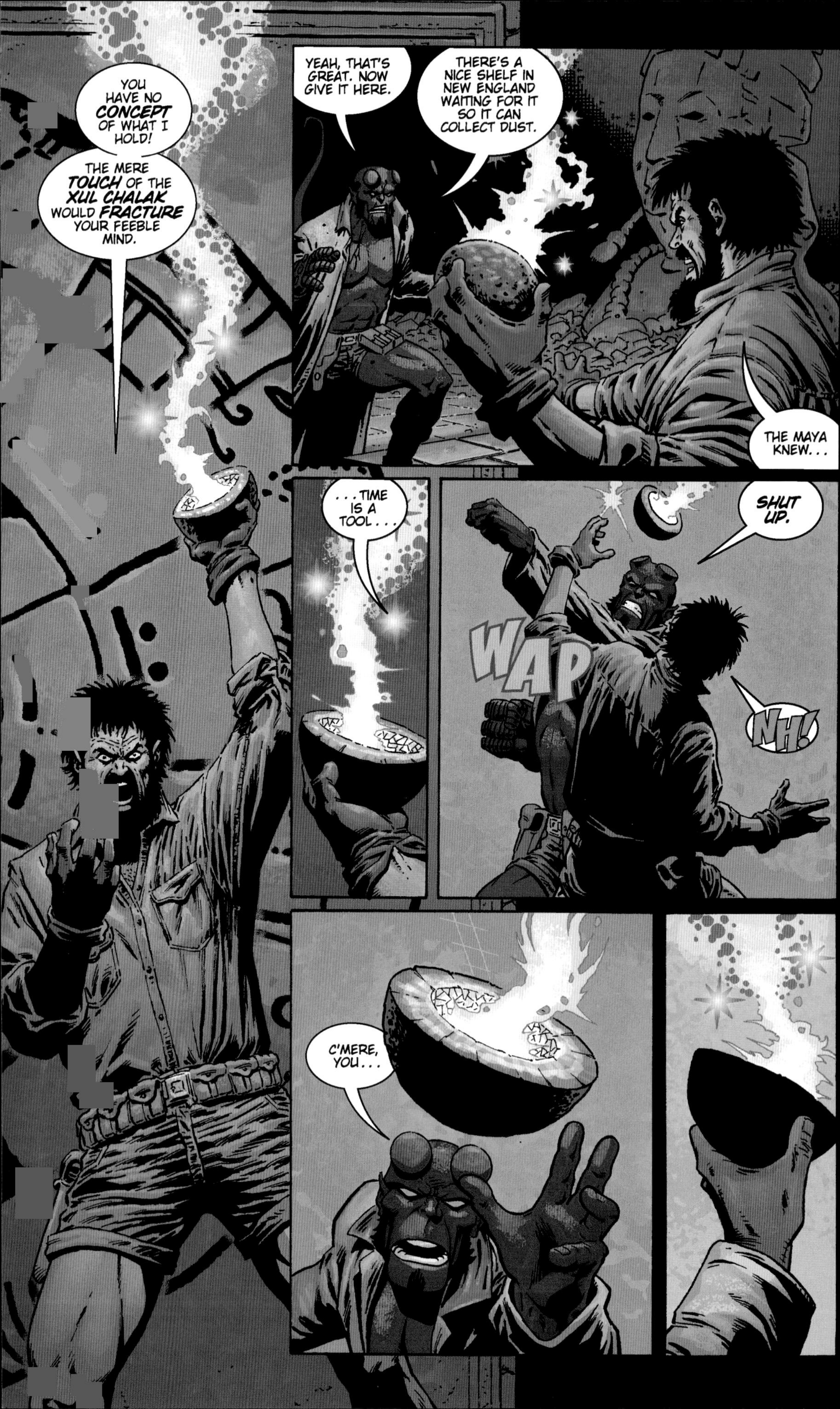

YOU HAVE NO ***CONCEPT*** OF WHAT I HOLD!
THE MERE ***TOUCH*** OF THE ***XUL CHALAK*** WOULD ***FRACTURE*** YOUR FEEBLE MIND.
YEAH, THAT'S GREAT. NOW GIVE IT HERE.
THERE'S A NICE SHELF IN NEW ENGLAND WAITING FOR IT SO IT CAN COLLECT DUST.
THE MAYA KNEW. . .
. . . TIME IS A TOOL . . .
SHUT UP.
WAP
NH!
C'MERE, YOU . . .

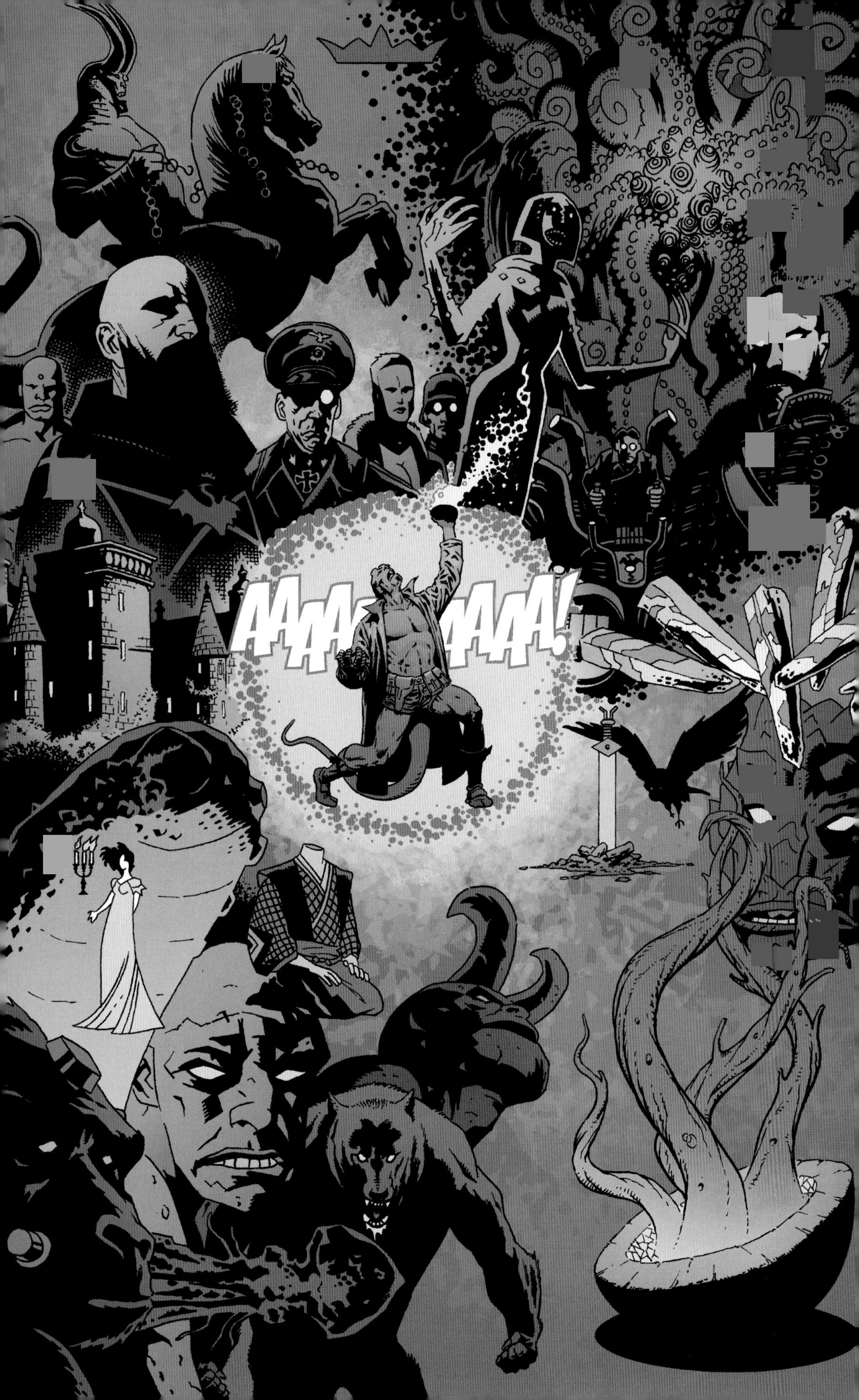
AAAAAAAA!

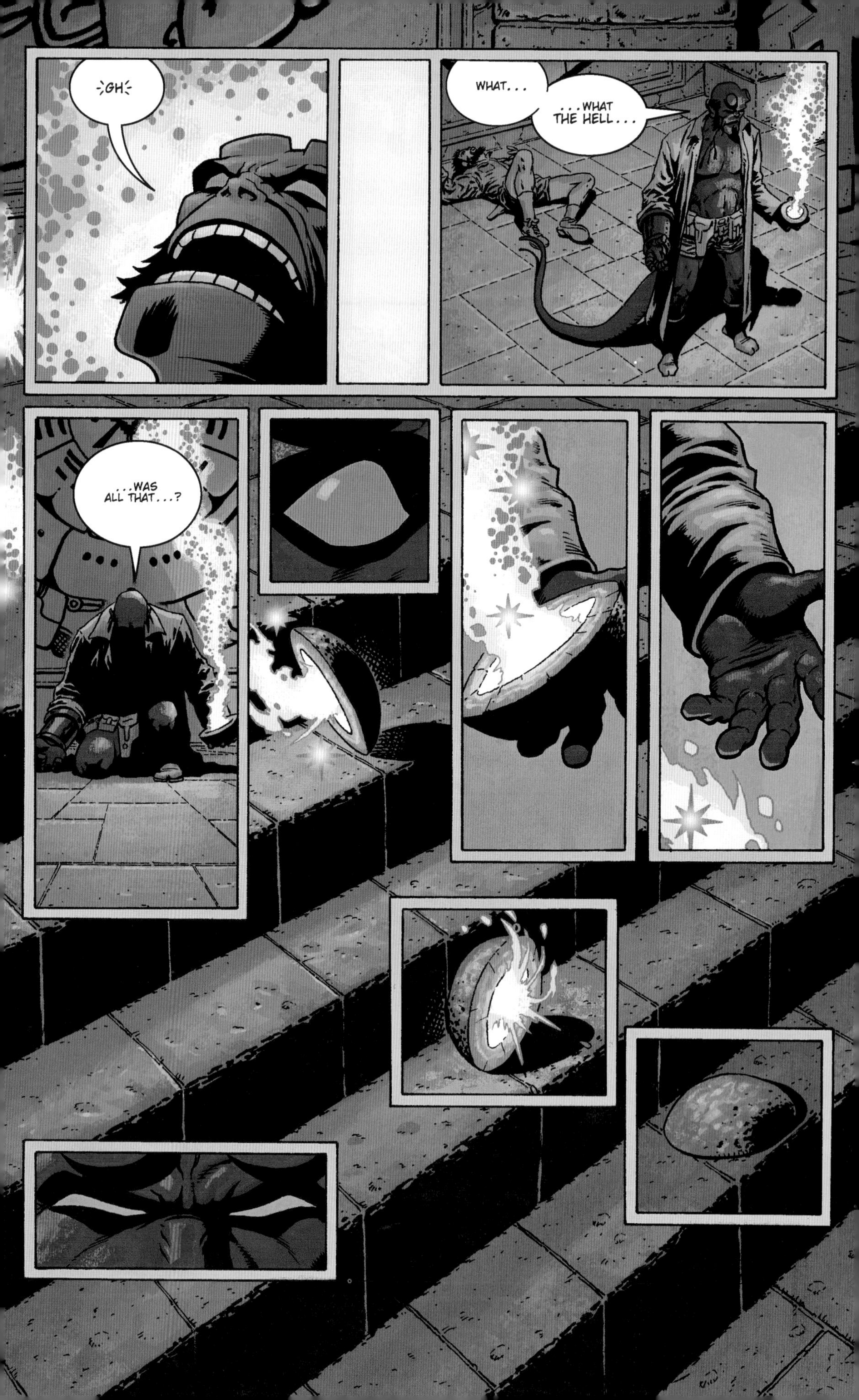
GH
WHAT. . .
. . .WHAT THE HELL. . .
. . .WAS ALL THAT. . .?

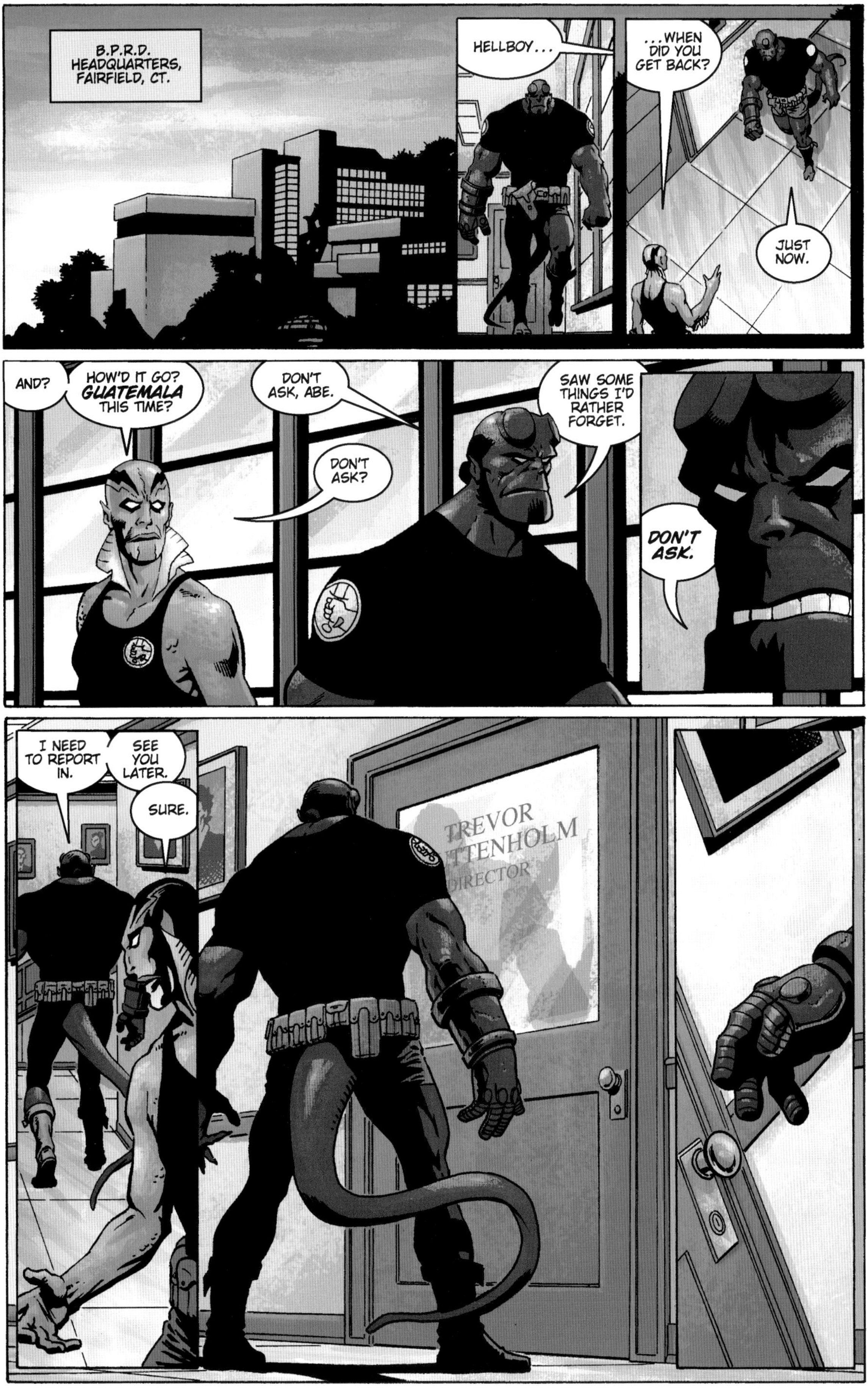
B.P.R.D. HEADQUARTERS, FAIRFIELD, CT.
HELLBOY...
...WHEN DID YOU GET BACK?
JUST NOW.
AND?
HOW'D IT GO? GUATEMALA THIS TIME?
DON'T ASK, ABE.
DON'T ASK?
SAW SOME THINGS I'D RATHER FORGET.
DON'T ASK.
I NEED TO REPORT IN.
SEE YOU LATER.
SURE.
TREVOR
TTENHOLM
DIRECTOR

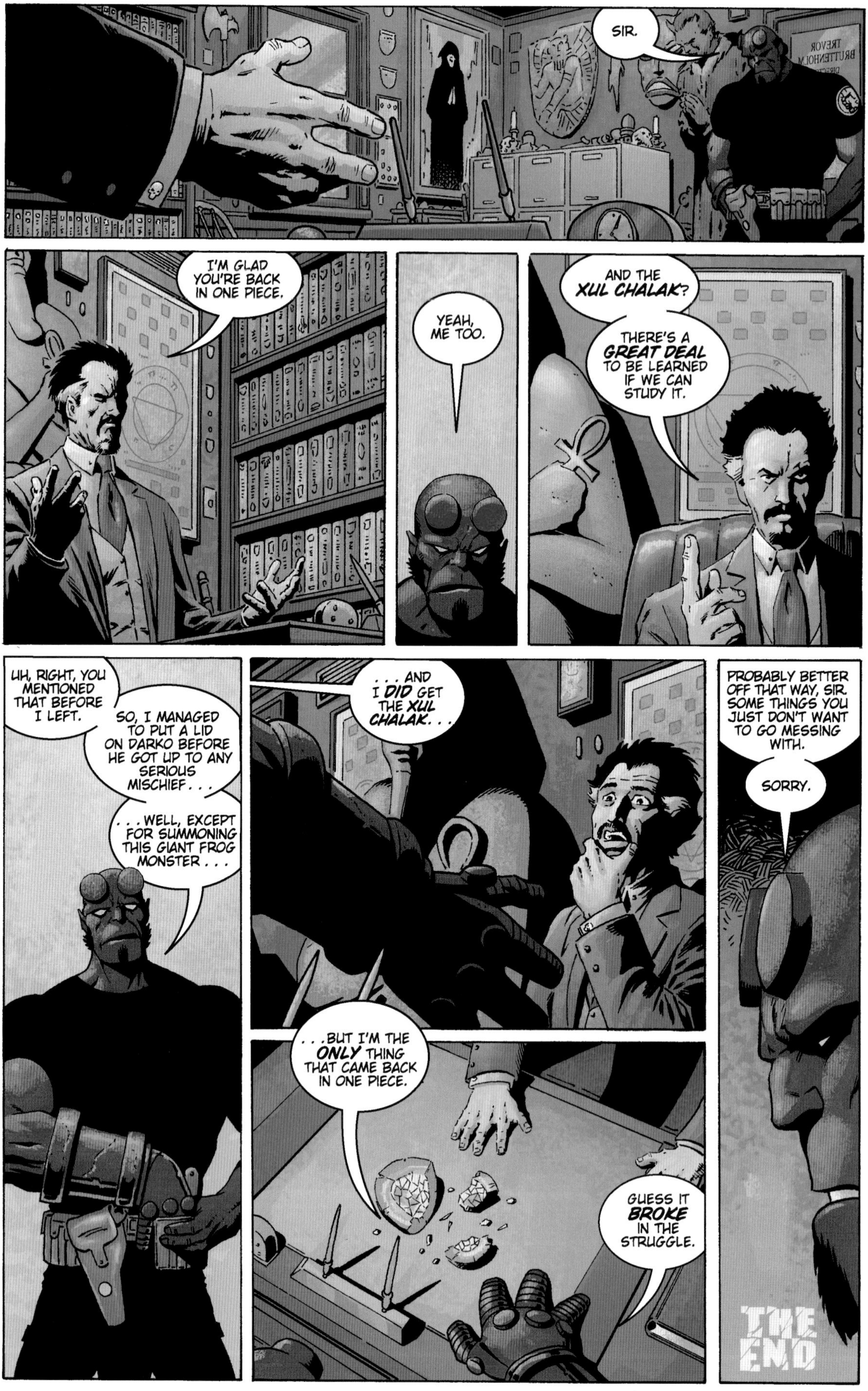

SIR.
TREVOR BRUTTENHOLM
I'M GLAD YOU'RE BACK IN ONE PIECE.
YEAH, ME TOO.
AND THE XUL CHALAK?
THERE'S A GREAT DEAL TO BE LEARNED IF WE CAN STUDY IT.
UH, RIGHT, YOU MENTIONED THAT BEFORE I LEFT.
SO, I MANAGED TO PUT A LID ON DARKO BEFORE HE GOT UP TO ANY SERIOUS MISCHIEF . . .
. . . WELL, EXCEPT FOR SUMMONING THIS GIANT FROG MONSTER . . .
. . . AND I DID GET THE XUL CHALAK . . .
. . .BUT I'M THE ONLY THING THAT CAME BACK IN ONE PIECE.
GUESS IT BROKE IN THE STRUGGLE.
PROBABLY BETTER OFF THAT WAY, SIR. SOME THINGS YOU JUST DON'T WANT TO GO MESSING WITH.
SORRY.
THE END

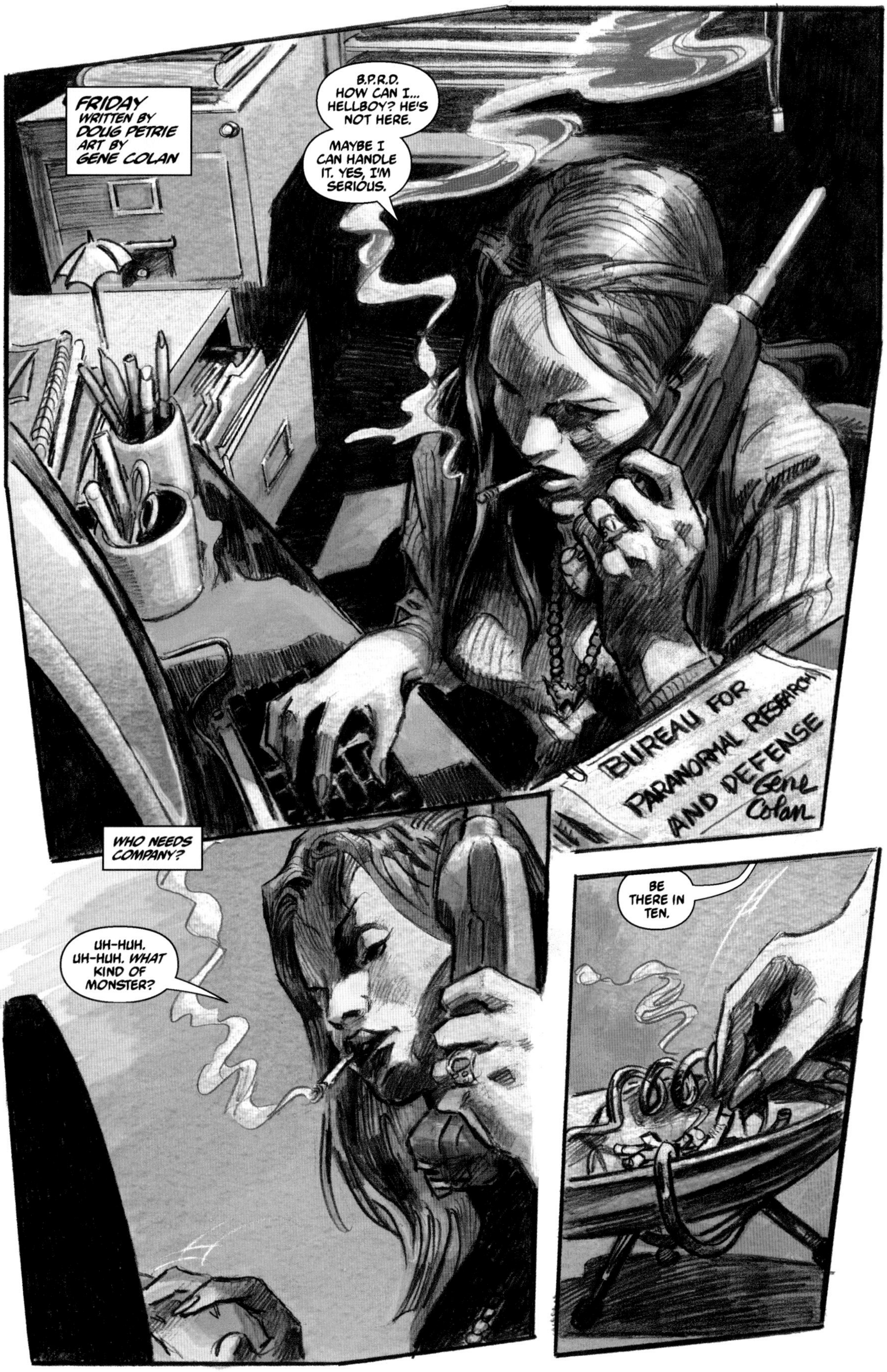
FRIDAY
WRITTEN BY DOUG PETRIE
ART BY GENE COLAN
B.P.R.D. HOW CAN I... HELLBOY? HE'S NOT HERE.
MAYBE I CAN HANDLE IT. YES, I'M SERIOUS.
BUREAU FOR PARANORMAL RESEARCH AND DEFENSE
Gene Colan
WHO NEEDS COMPANY?
UH-HUH. UH-HUH. WHAT KIND OF MONSTER?
BE THERE IN TEN.

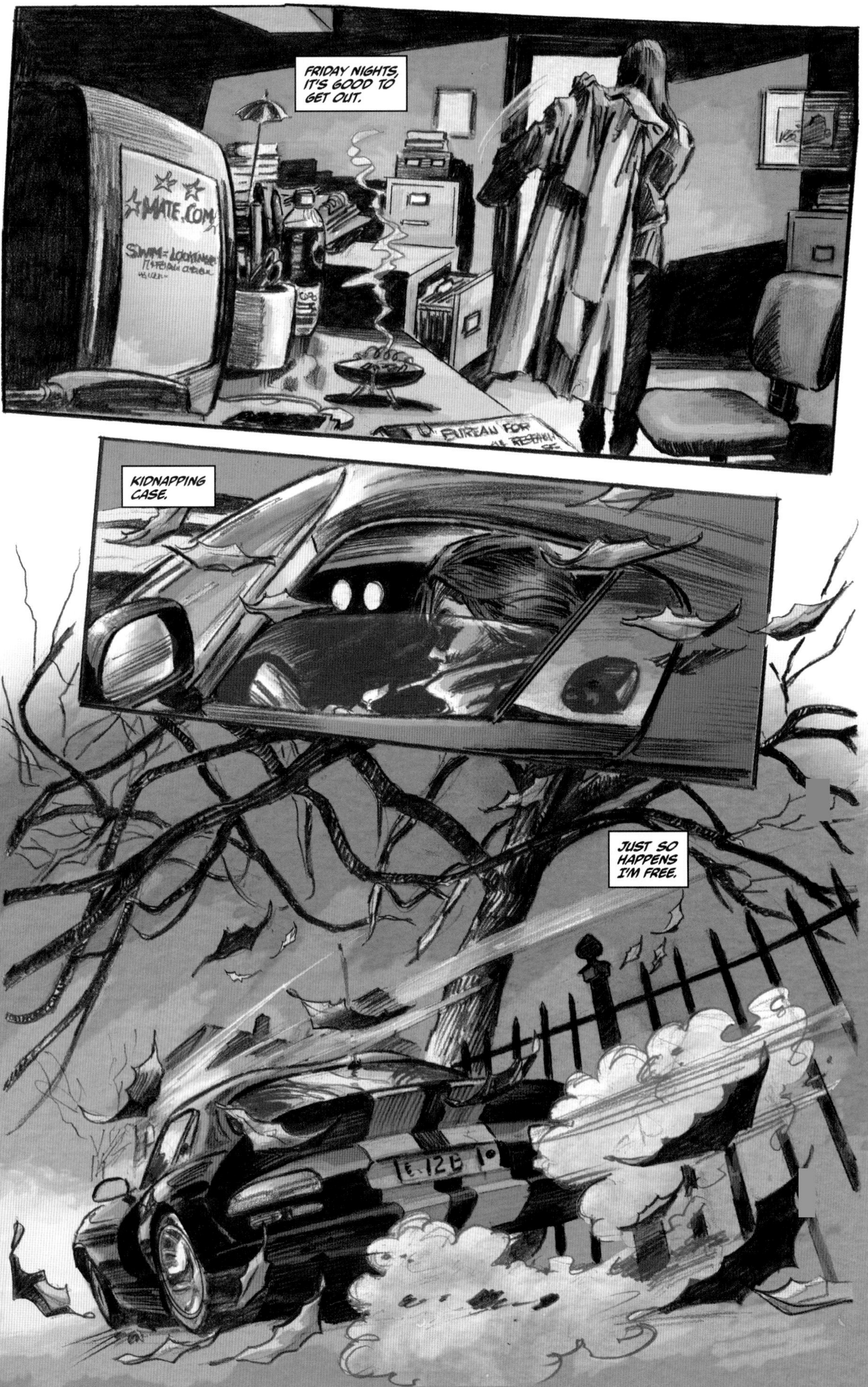
FRIDAY NIGHTS, IT'S GOOD TO GET OUT.
KIDNAPPING CASE.
JUST SO HAPPENS I'M FREE.

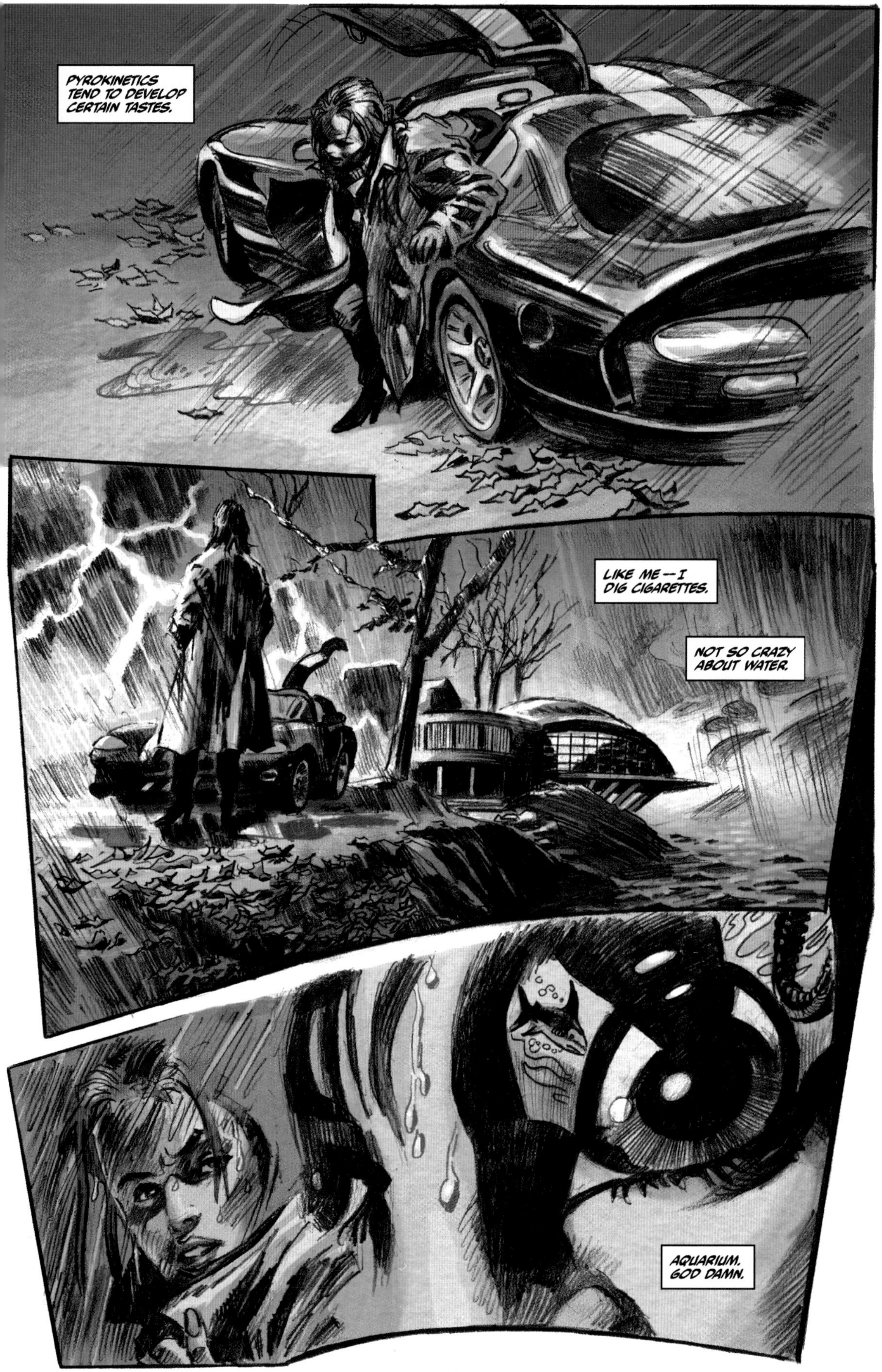
PYROKINETICS TEND TO DEVELOP CERTAIN TASTES.
LIKE ME -- I DIG CIGARETTES.
NOT SO CRAZY ABOUT WATER.
AQUARIUM. GOD DAMN.

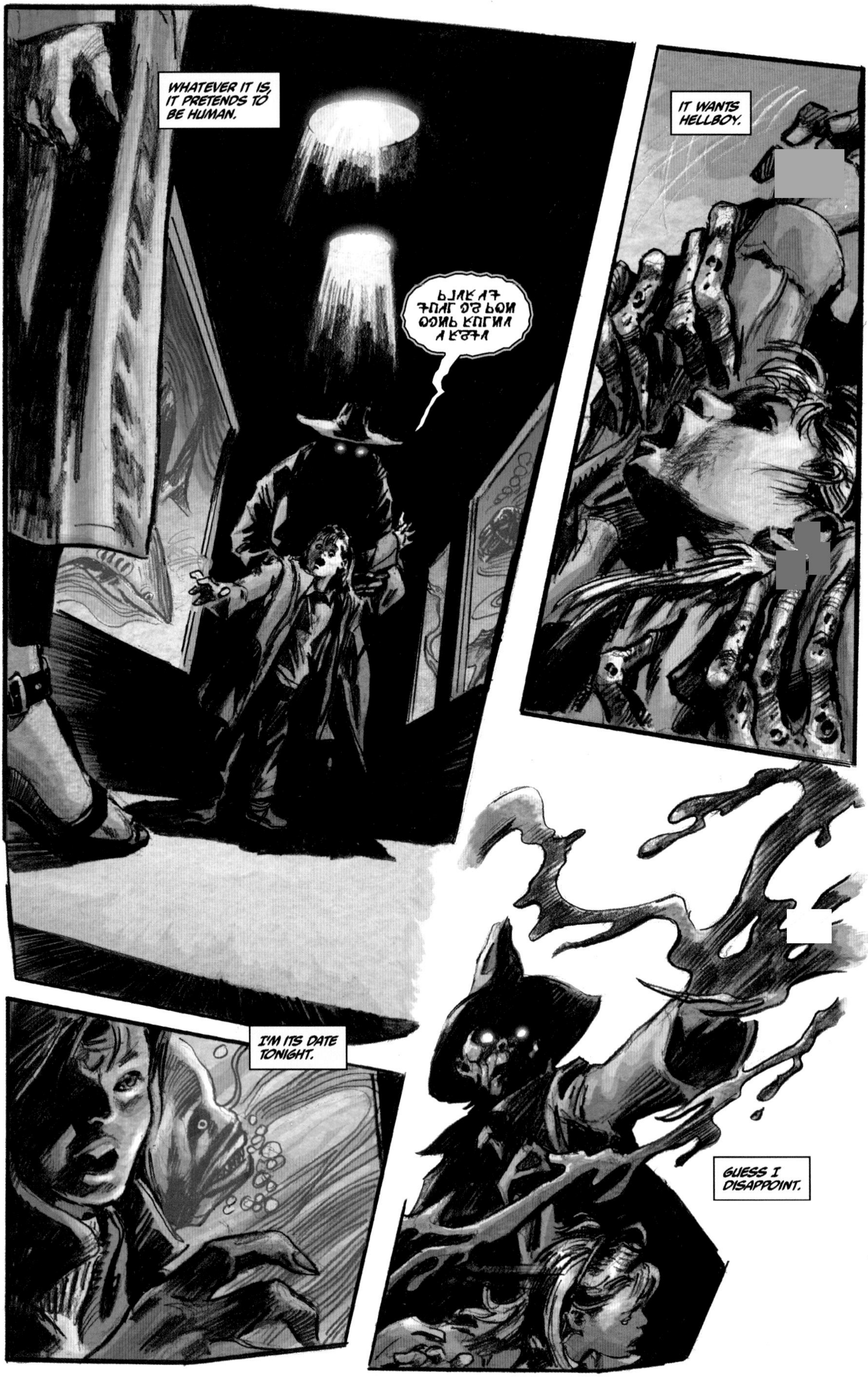
WHATEVER IT IS, IT PRETENDS TO BE HUMAN.
IT WANTS HELLBOY.
I'M ITS DATE TONIGHT.
GUESS I DISAPPOINT.

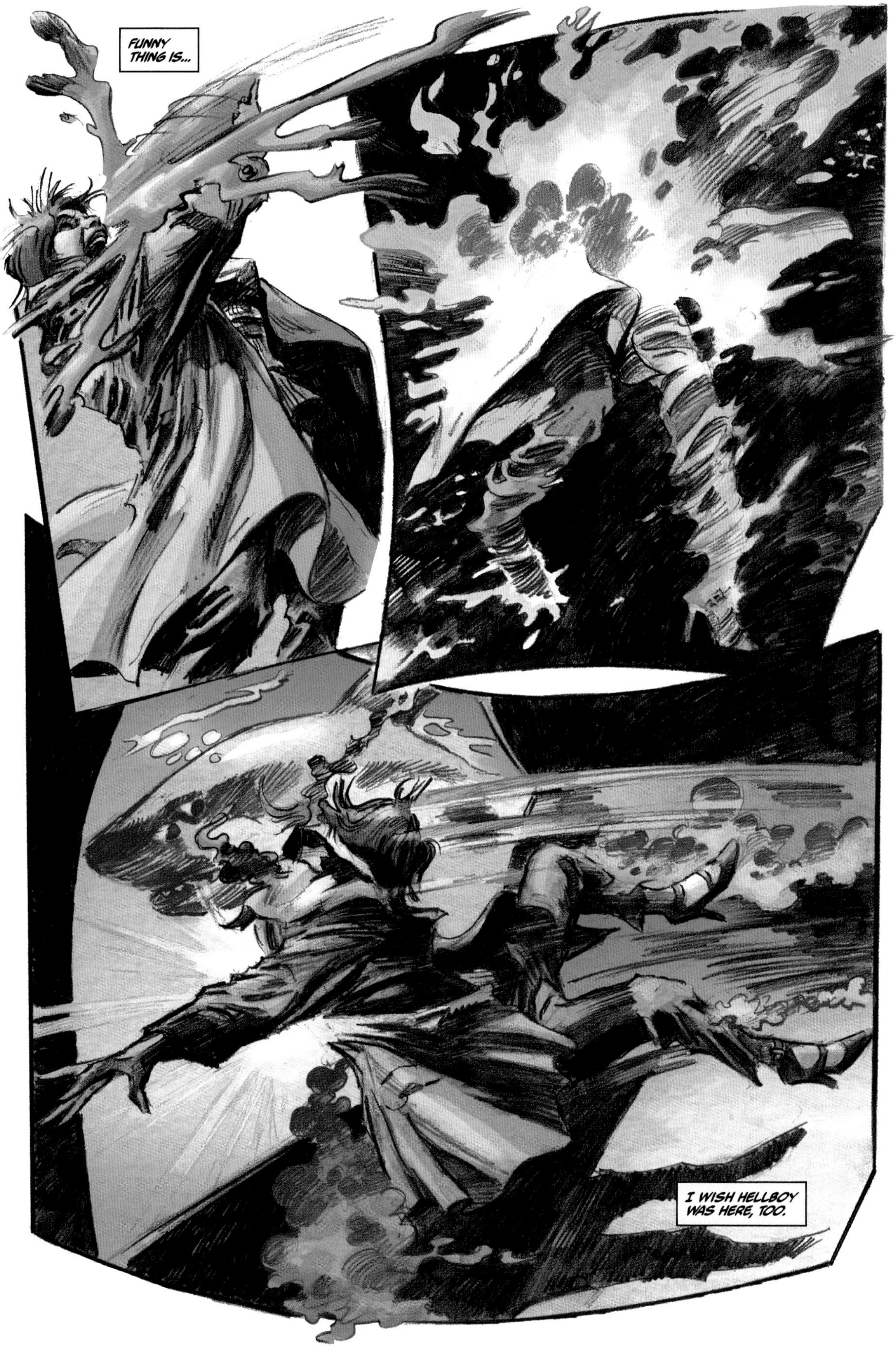
FUNNY THING IS...
I WISH HELLBOY WAS HERE, TOO.

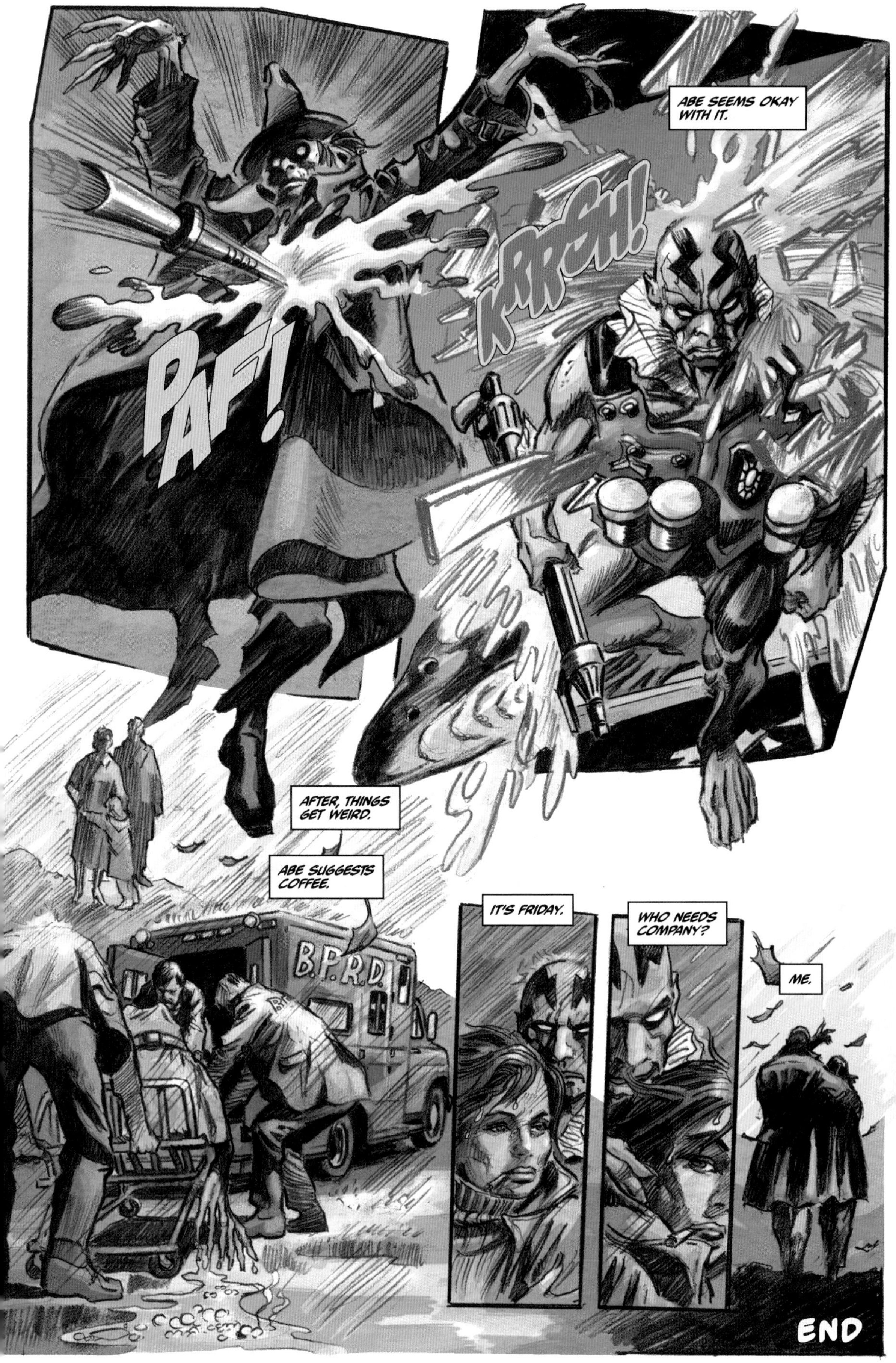
ABE SEEMS OKAY WITH IT.
KRRSH!
PAF!
AFTER, THINGS GET WEIRD.
ABE SUGGESTS COFFEE.
B.P.R.D.
IT'S FRIDAY.
WHO NEEDS COMPANY?
ME.
END

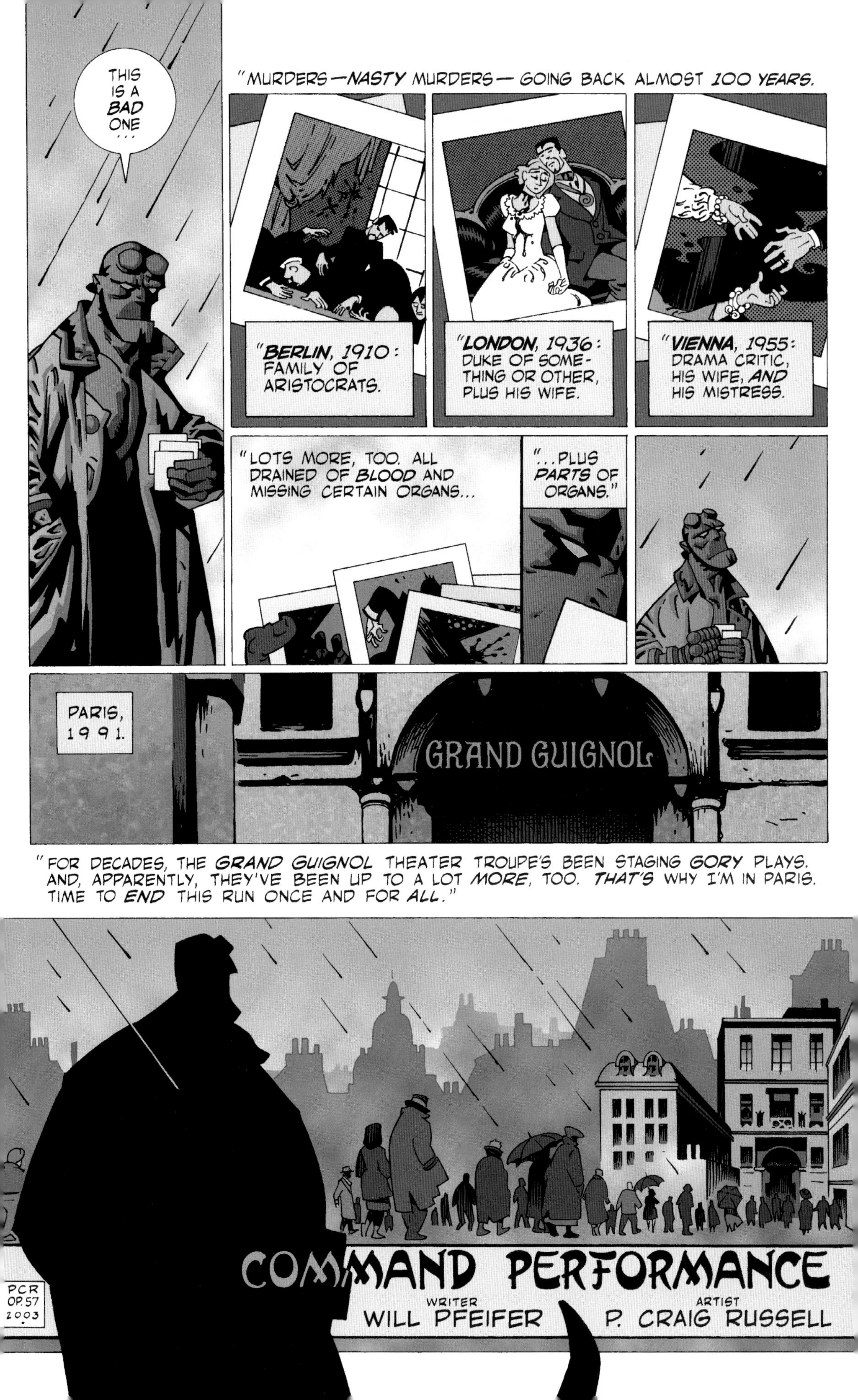

THIS IS A BAD ONE . . .
"MURDERS—NASTY MURDERS— GOING BACK ALMOST 100 YEARS.
"BERLIN, 1910: FAMILY OF ARISTOCRATS.
"LONDON, 1936: DUKE OF SOME-THING OR OTHER, PLUS HIS WIFE.
"VIENNA, 1955: DRAMA CRITIC, HIS WIFE, AND HIS MISTRESS.
"LOTS MORE, TOO. ALL DRAINED OF BLOOD AND MISSING CERTAIN ORGANS...
"...PLUS PARTS OF ORGANS."
PARIS, 1991.
GRAND GUIGNOL
"FOR DECADES, THE GRAND GUIGNOL THEATER TROUPE'S BEEN STAGING GORY PLAYS. AND, APPARENTLY, THEY'VE BEEN UP TO A LOT MORE, TOO. THAT'S WHY I'M IN PARIS. TIME TO END THIS RUN ONCE AND FOR ALL."
COMMAND PERFORMANCE
WRITER WILL PFEIFER
ARTIST P. CRAIG RUSSELL
PCR OP.57 2003

I'M *SURPRISED* YOU KNOW WHO I AM. THE *BUREAU* USUALLY KEEPS THINGS PRETTY QUIET.

IN *OUR* LINE OF WORK, WE COME TO POSSESS ALL *MANNER* OF INTRIGUING INFORMATION.

OUR CLIENTELE IS RATHER, SHALL WE SAY, *DEDICATED*...

...AND THEY'RE ALWAYS GRATEFUL FOR THE *UNIQUE* BRAND OF THEATRICS WE PROVIDE.

SO YOU GUYS *STILL* DRAW AN AUDIENCE, EH? I THOUGHT *SLASHER* MOVIES AND VIDEO GAMES WOULD'VE *TAKEN* YOUR PLACE.

CREEEEEK

OH, THERE'S ALWAYS A MARKET FOR THE *GRAND GUIGNOL*, HELLBOY. SOME PEOPLE DEMAND THE...*IMMEDIACY*. IT'S BEEN THAT WAY FOR *MORE* THAN A CENTURY.

SINCE YOUR *ANCESTORS* STARTED THIS RACKET, RIGHT, ANDRÉ?

ER, YES, THAT'S RIGHT, HELLBOY. BUT IF YOU'LL *EXCUSE* US, IT'S TIME FOR THE *SHOW*.

38

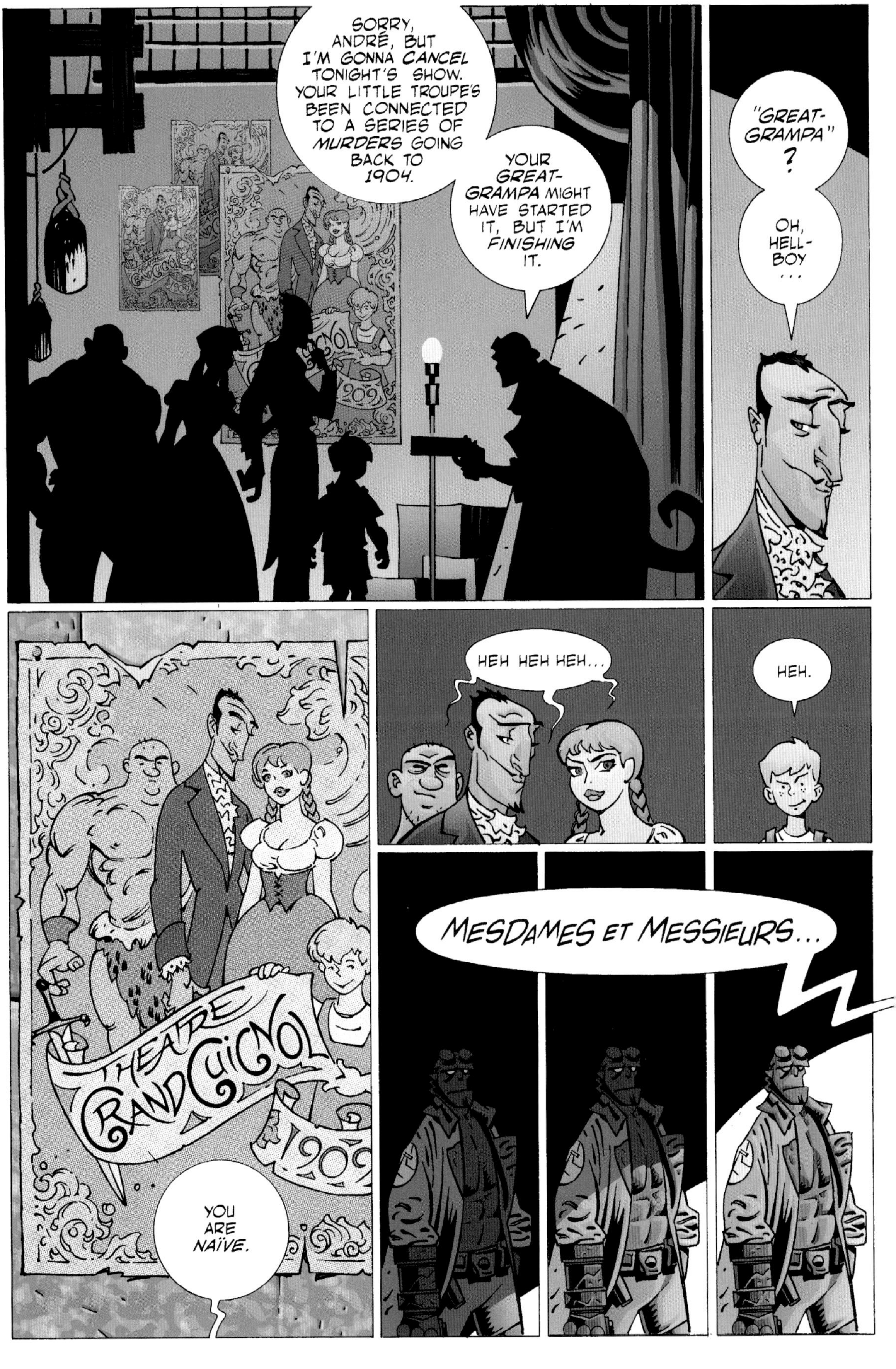
SORRY, ANDRÉ, BUT I'M GONNA CANCEL TONIGHT'S SHOW. YOUR LITTLE TROUPE'S BEEN CONNECTED TO A SERIES OF MURDERS GOING BACK TO 1904.
YOUR GREAT-GRAMPA MIGHT HAVE STARTED IT, BUT I'M FINISHING IT.
"GREAT-GRAMPA" ?
OH, HELL-BOY . . .
THEATRE GRAND GUIGNOL 1909
YOU ARE NAÏVE.
HEH HEH HEH...
HEH.
MESDAMES ET MESSIEURS...

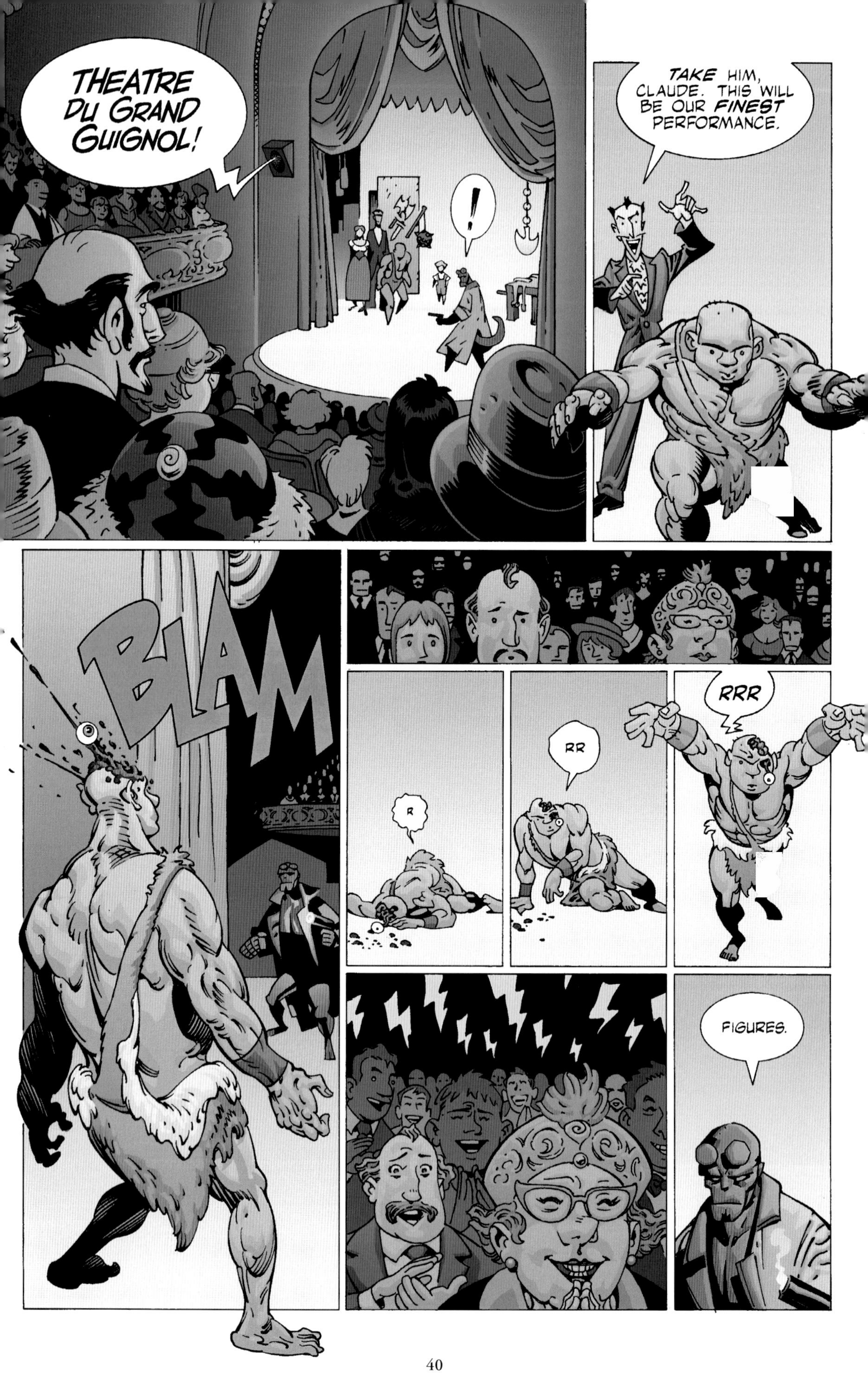
THEATRE DU GRAND GUIGNOL!
!
TAKE HIM, CLAUDE. THIS WILL BE OUR FINEST PERFORMANCE.
BLAM
R
RR
RRR
FIGURES.

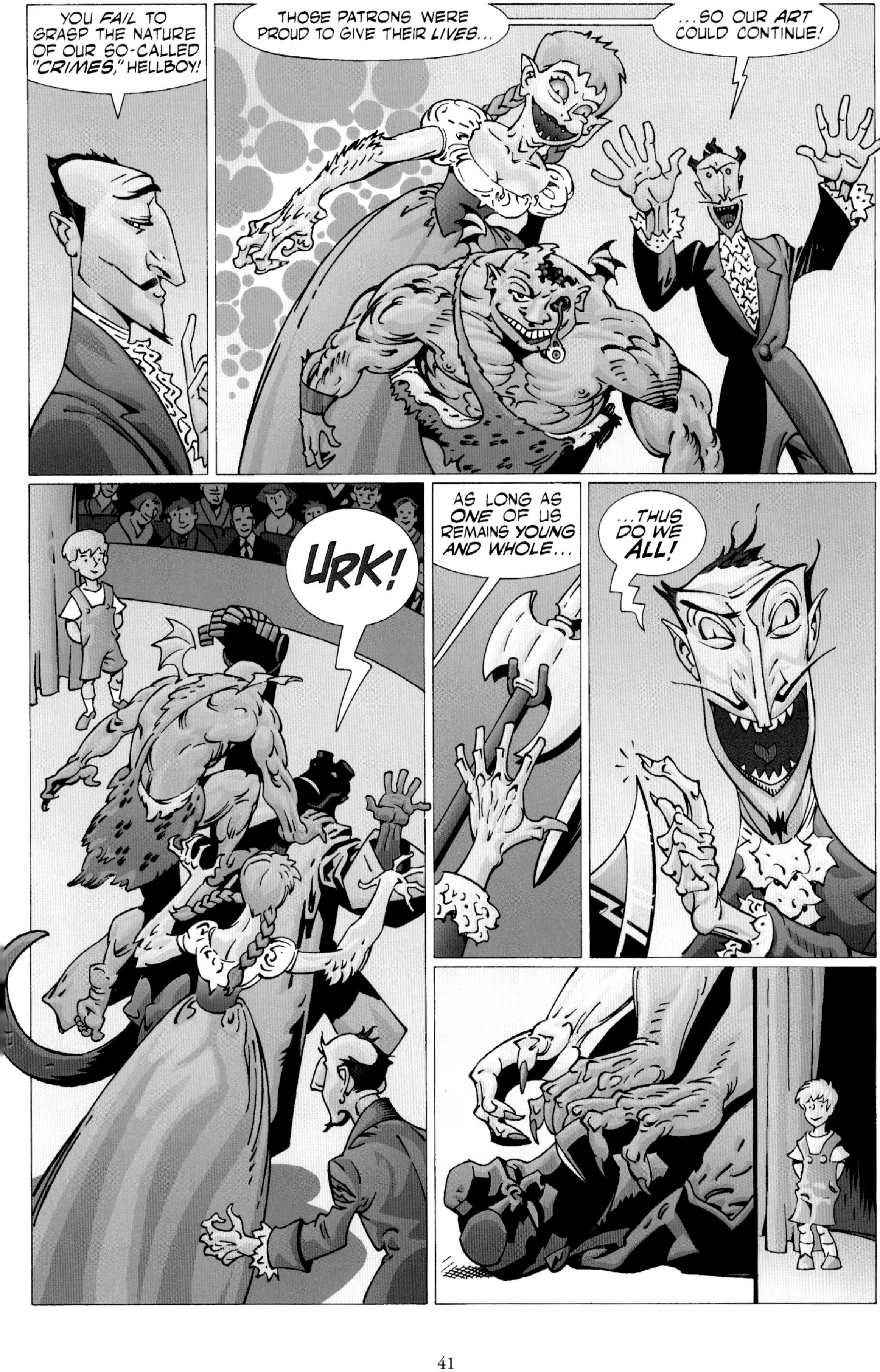
YOU FAIL TO GRASP THE NATURE OF OUR SO-CALLED "CRIMES," HELLBOY!
THOSE PATRONS WERE PROUD TO GIVE THEIR LIVES...
...SO OUR ART COULD CONTINUE!
URK!
AS LONG AS ONE OF US REMAINS YOUNG AND WHOLE...
...THUS DO WE ALL!

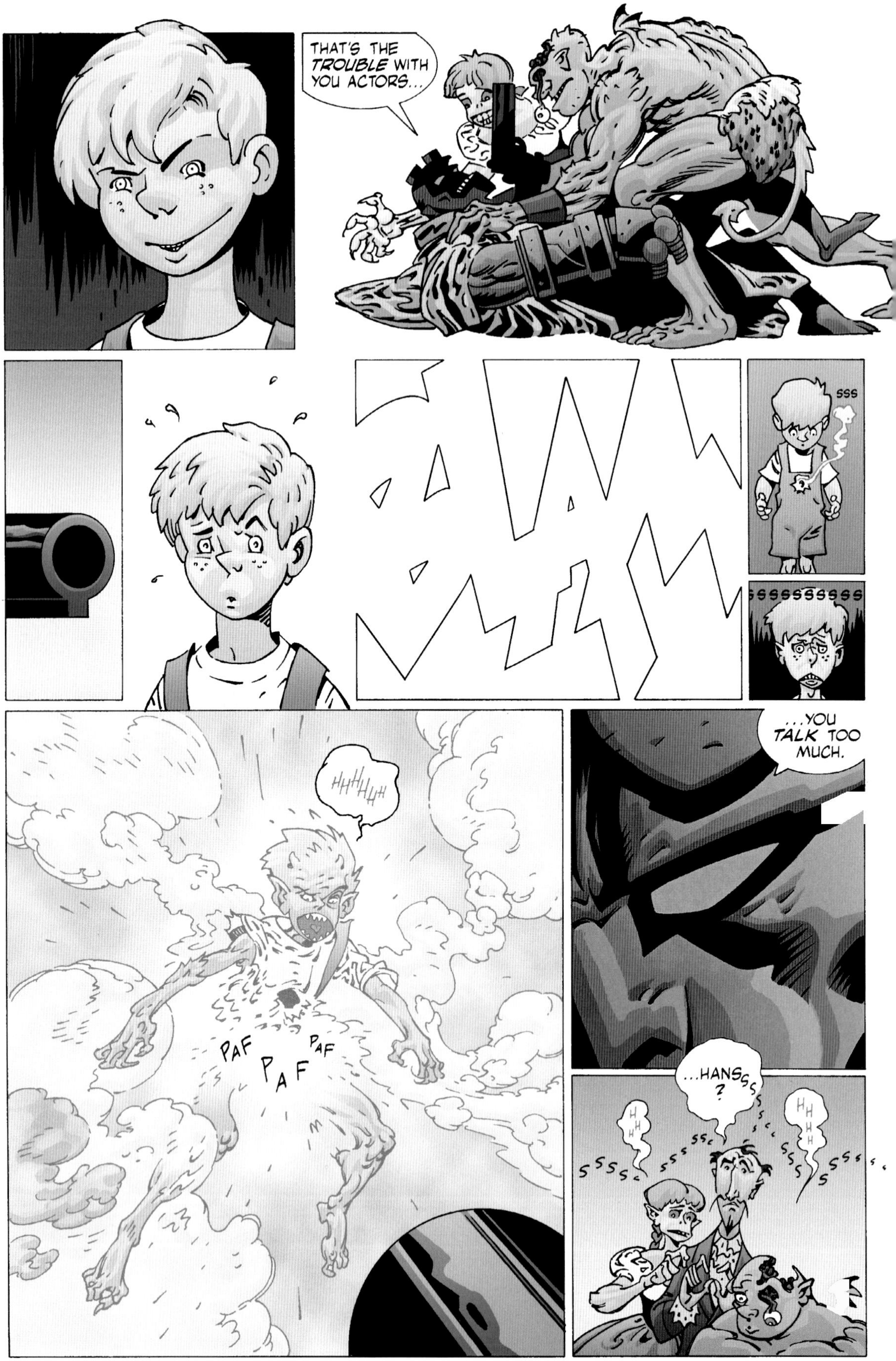
THAT'S THE TROUBLE WITH YOU ACTORS...
SSS
SSSSSSSSSS
HHHHHH
PAF
PAF
PAF
...YOU TALK TOO MUCH.
...HANS?

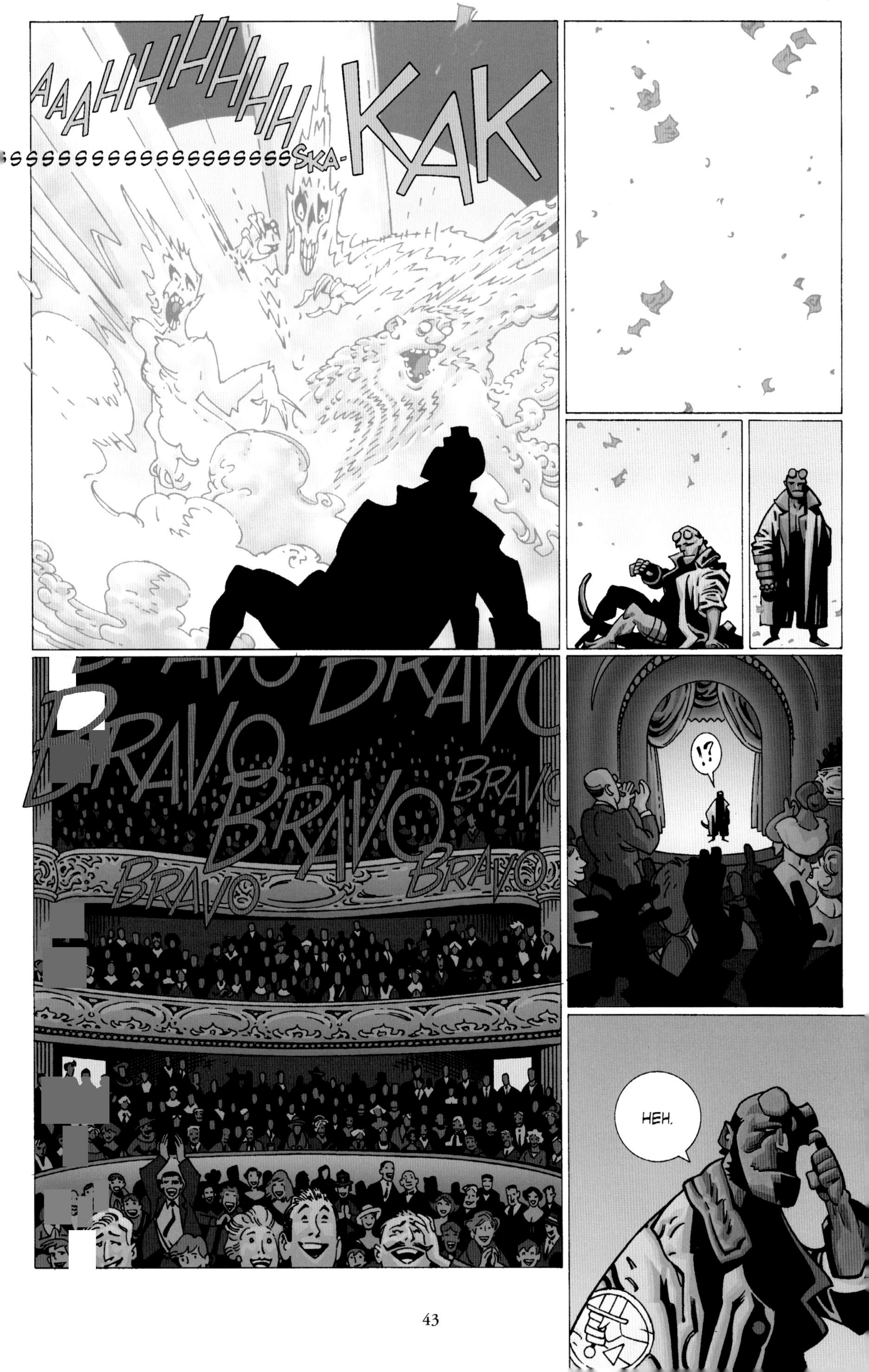
AAAHHHHHHHH
SSSSSSSSSSSSSSSSSSSSKA-KAK
BRAVO BRAVO BRAVO BRAVO BRAVO BRAVO BRAVO BRAVO
!?
HEH.

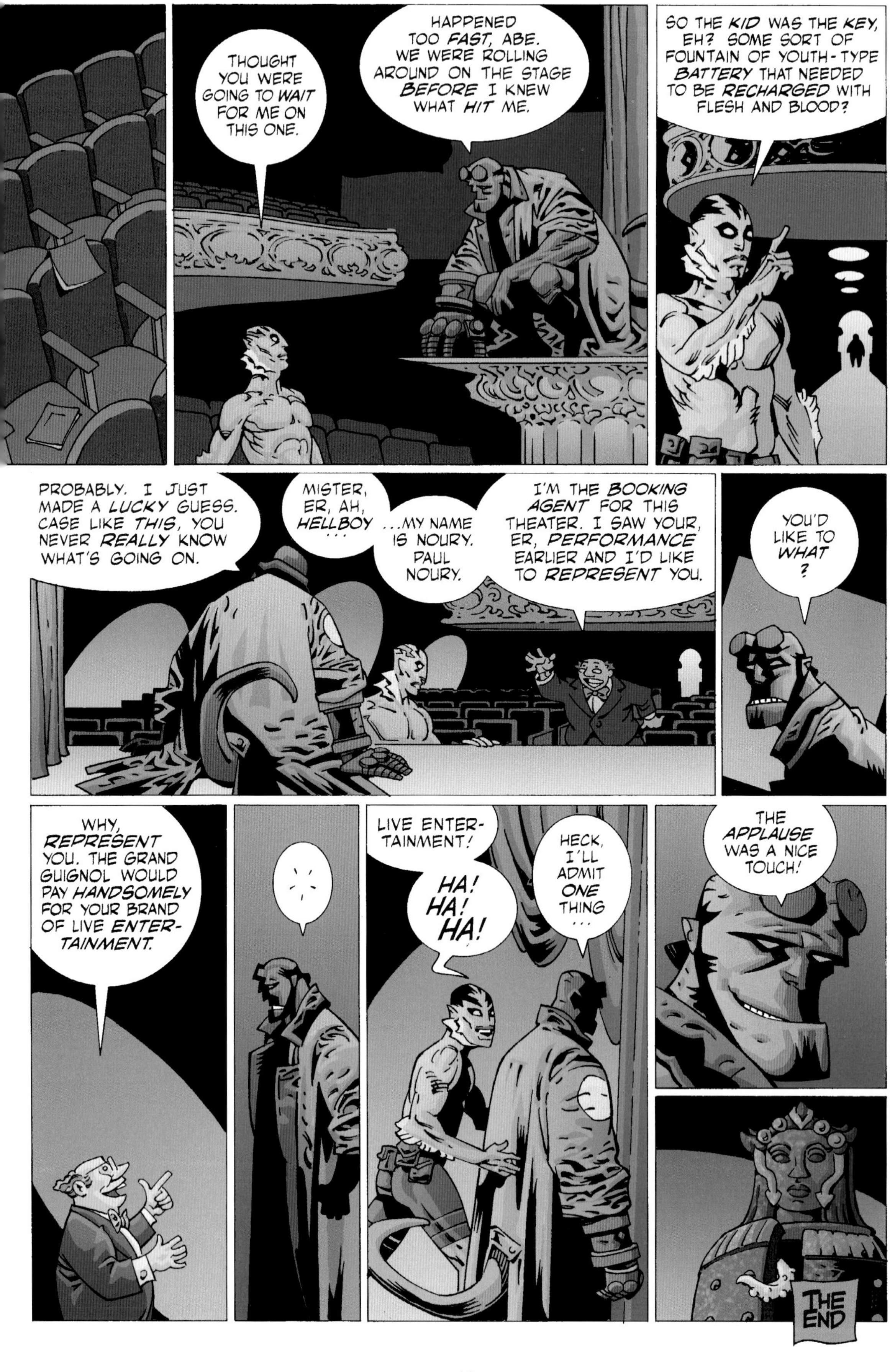
THOUGHT YOU WERE GOING TO WAIT FOR ME ON THIS ONE.
HAPPENED TOO FAST, ABE. WE WERE ROLLING AROUND ON THE STAGE BEFORE I KNEW WHAT HIT ME.
SO THE KID WAS THE KEY, EH? SOME SORT OF FOUNTAIN OF YOUTH-TYPE BATTERY THAT NEEDED TO BE RECHARGED WITH FLESH AND BLOOD?
PROBABLY. I JUST MADE A LUCKY GUESS. CASE LIKE THIS, YOU NEVER REALLY KNOW WHAT'S GOING ON.
MISTER, ER, AH, HELLBOY . . .
. . .MY NAME IS NOURY. PAUL NOURY.
I'M THE BOOKING AGENT FOR THIS THEATER. I SAW YOUR, ER, PERFORMANCE EARLIER AND I'D LIKE TO REPRESENT YOU.
YOU'D LIKE TO WHAT ?
WHY, REPRESENT YOU. THE GRAND GUIGNOL WOULD PAY HANDSOMELY FOR YOUR BRAND OF LIVE ENTERTAINMENT.
LIVE ENTERTAINMENT!
HA! HA! HA!
HECK, I'LL ADMIT ONE THING . . .
THE APPLAUSE WAS A NICE TOUCH!
THE END

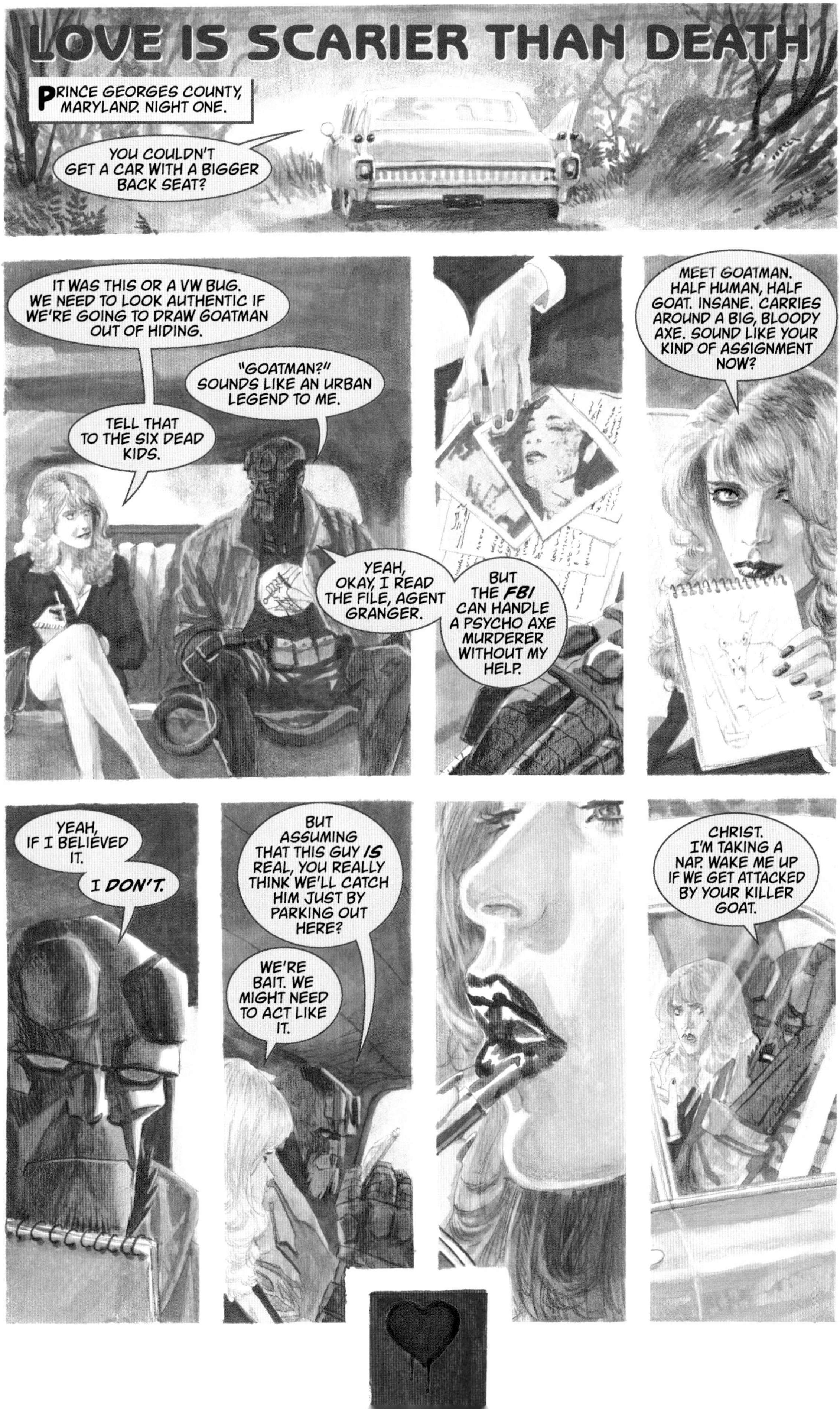
LOVE IS SCARIER THAN DEATH
PRINCE GEORGES COUNTY, MARYLAND. NIGHT ONE.
YOU COULDN'T GET A CAR WITH A BIGGER BACK SEAT?
IT WAS THIS OR A VW BUG. WE NEED TO LOOK AUTHENTIC IF WE'RE GOING TO DRAW GOATMAN OUT OF HIDING.
"GOATMAN?" SOUNDS LIKE AN URBAN LEGEND TO ME.
TELL THAT TO THE SIX DEAD KIDS.
YEAH, OKAY, I READ THE FILE, AGENT GRANGER.
BUT THE FBI CAN HANDLE A PSYCHO AXE MURDERER WITHOUT MY HELP.
MEET GOATMAN. HALF HUMAN, HALF GOAT. INSANE. CARRIES AROUND A BIG, BLOODY AXE. SOUND LIKE YOUR KIND OF ASSIGNMENT NOW?
YEAH, IF I BELIEVED IT.
I DON'T.
BUT ASSUMING THAT THIS GUY IS REAL, YOU REALLY THINK WE'LL CATCH HIM JUST BY PARKING OUT HERE?
WE'RE BAIT. WE MIGHT NEED TO ACT LIKE IT.
CHRIST. I'M TAKING A NAP. WAKE ME UP IF WE GET ATTACKED BY YOUR KILLER GOAT.

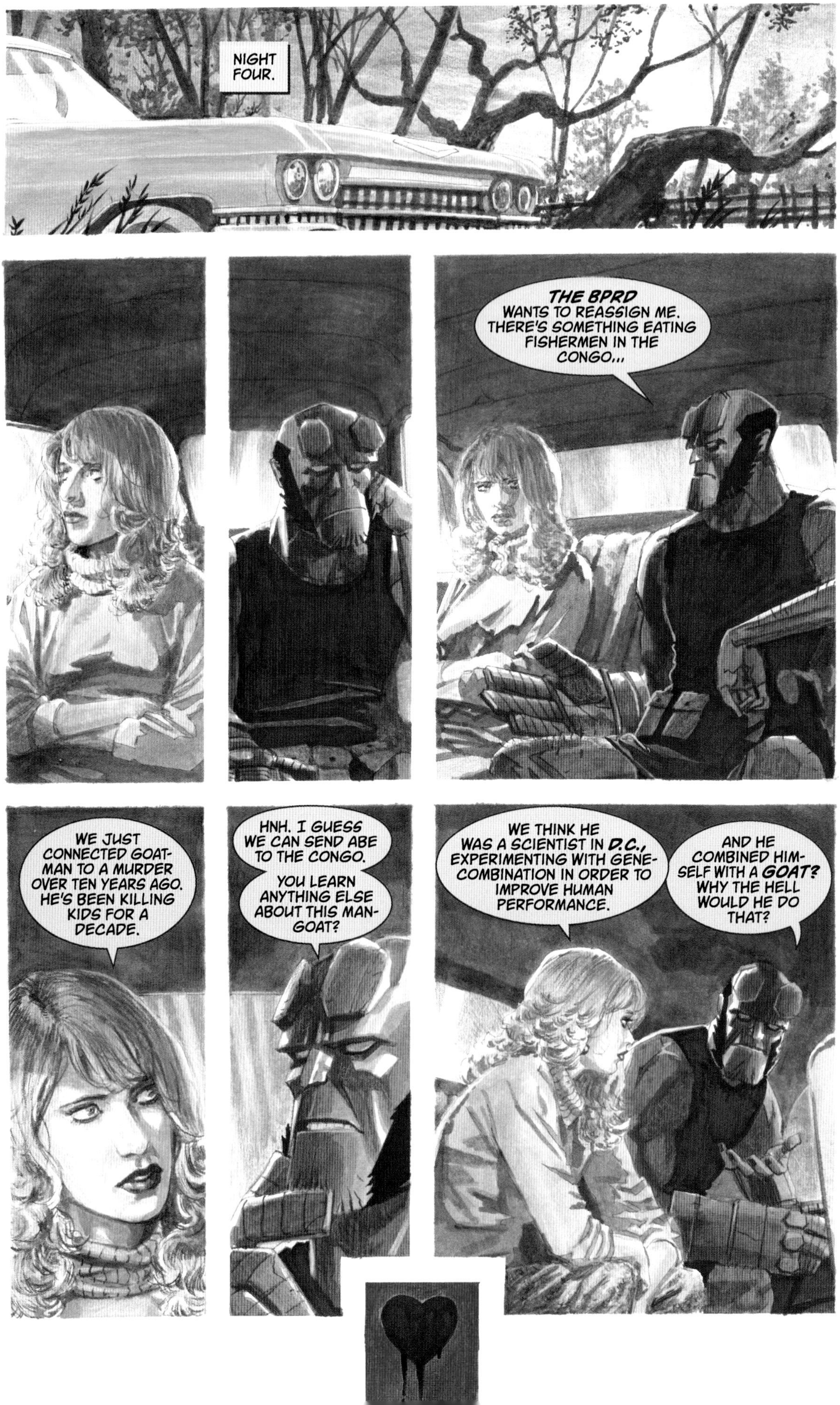
NIGHT FOUR.
THE BPRD WANTS TO REASSIGN ME. THERE'S SOMETHING EATING FISHERMEN IN THE CONGO...
WE JUST CONNECTED GOAT-MAN TO A MURDER OVER TEN YEARS AGO. HE'S BEEN KILLING KIDS FOR A DECADE.
HNH. I GUESS WE CAN SEND ABE TO THE CONGO.
YOU LEARN ANYTHING ELSE ABOUT THIS MAN-GOAT?
WE THINK HE WAS A SCIENTIST IN D.C., EXPERIMENTING WITH GENE-COMBINATION IN ORDER TO IMPROVE HUMAN PERFORMANCE.
AND HE COMBINED HIM-SELF WITH A GOAT? WHY THE HELL WOULD HE DO THAT?

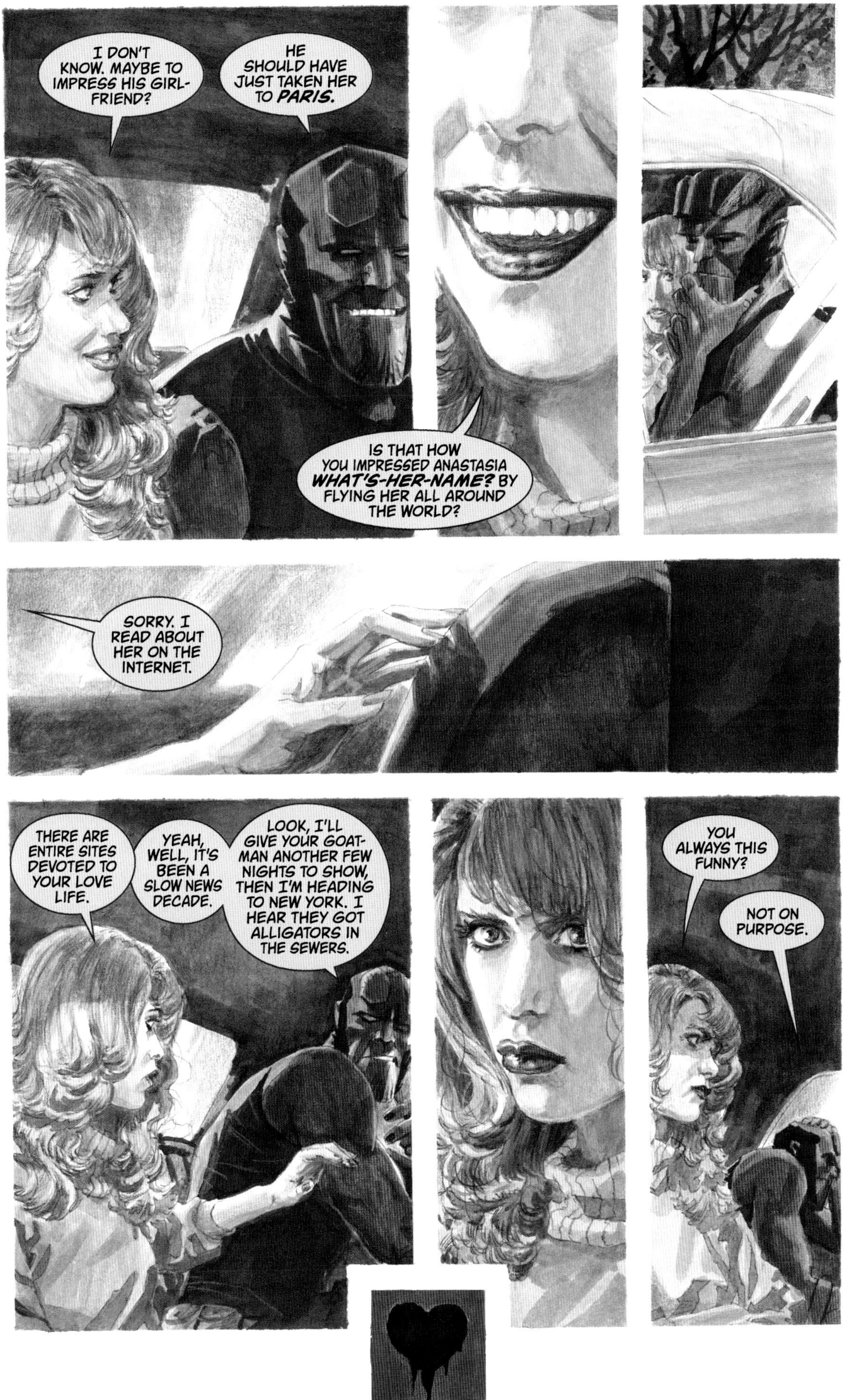
I DON'T KNOW. MAYBE TO IMPRESS HIS GIRL-FRIEND?
HE SHOULD HAVE JUST TAKEN HER TO PARIS.
IS THAT HOW YOU IMPRESSED ANASTASIA WHAT'S-HER-NAME? BY FLYING HER ALL AROUND THE WORLD?
SORRY. I READ ABOUT HER ON THE INTERNET.
THERE ARE ENTIRE SITES DEVOTED TO YOUR LOVE LIFE.
YEAH, WELL, IT'S BEEN A SLOW NEWS DECADE.
LOOK, I'LL GIVE YOUR GOAT-MAN ANOTHER FEW NIGHTS TO SHOW, THEN I'M HEADING TO NEW YORK. I HEAR THEY GOT ALLIGATORS IN THE SEWERS.
YOU ALWAYS THIS FUNNY?
NOT ON PURPOSE.

NIGHT SEVEN.

THANKS FOR DINNER.

NO WORRIES. I FIGURED IT WAS FINALLY MY TURN TO PAY.

IT'S BEEN A WEEK, EMMA.

I KNOW. I'M SORRY, BUT...

OKAY, I'M JUST GOING TO PUT THIS OUT THERE. GOAT-MAN'S VICTIMS WERE ALWAYS COUPLES IN THE THROES OF *PASSION.*

MAYBE HE WAS DRAWN BY THEIR RAGING HORMONES, OR SOME PRIMAL ENERGY THAT THEY RELEASED. BUT WHATEVER SIGNAL THEY SENT, *WE'RE* NOT SENDING...

OH, COME ON...GOATMAN ISN'T EVEN *REAL!*

THEN WE WON'T BE *INTERRUPTED.* WHERE'S THE PROBLEM?

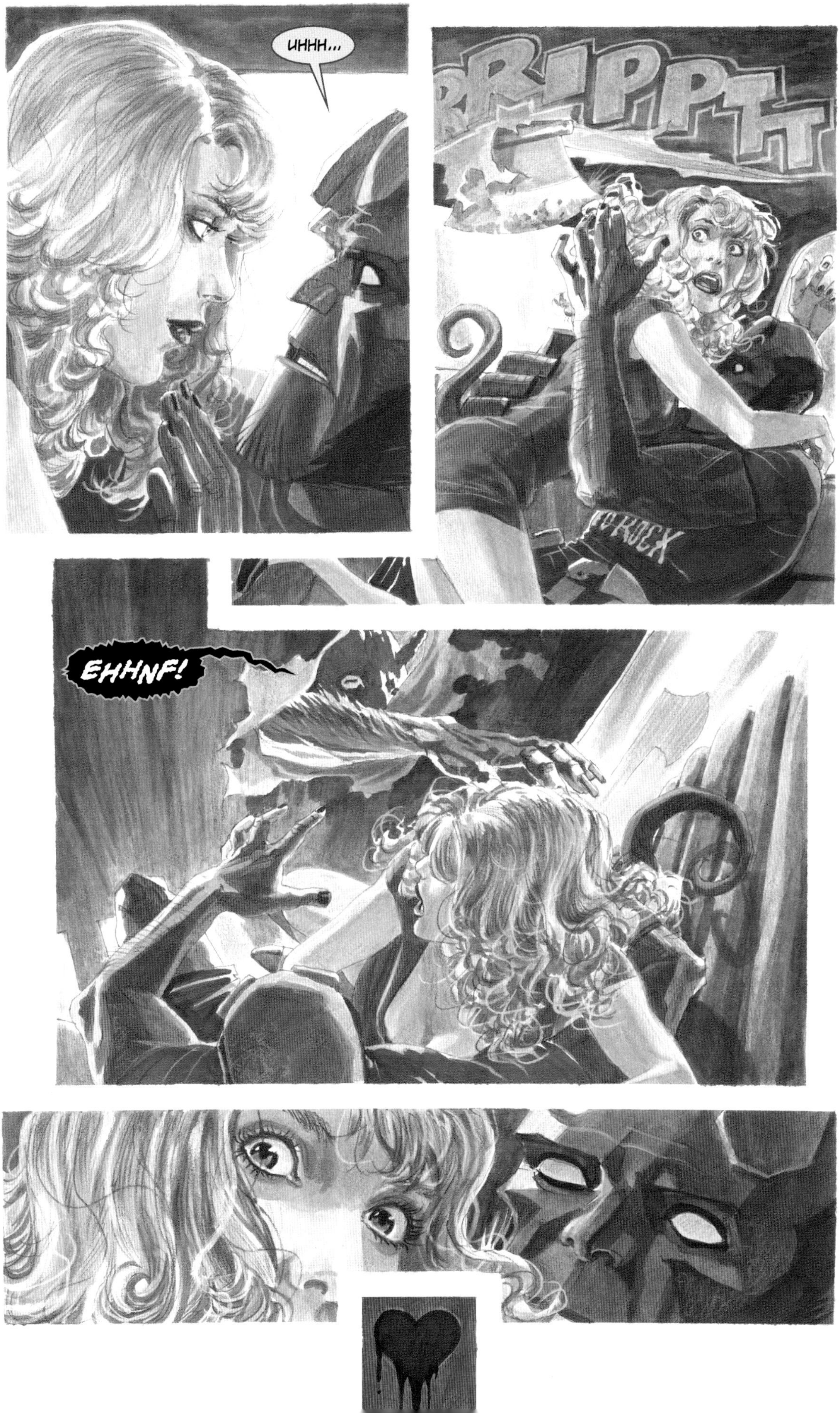
UHHH...
RRIPPTT
EHHNF!

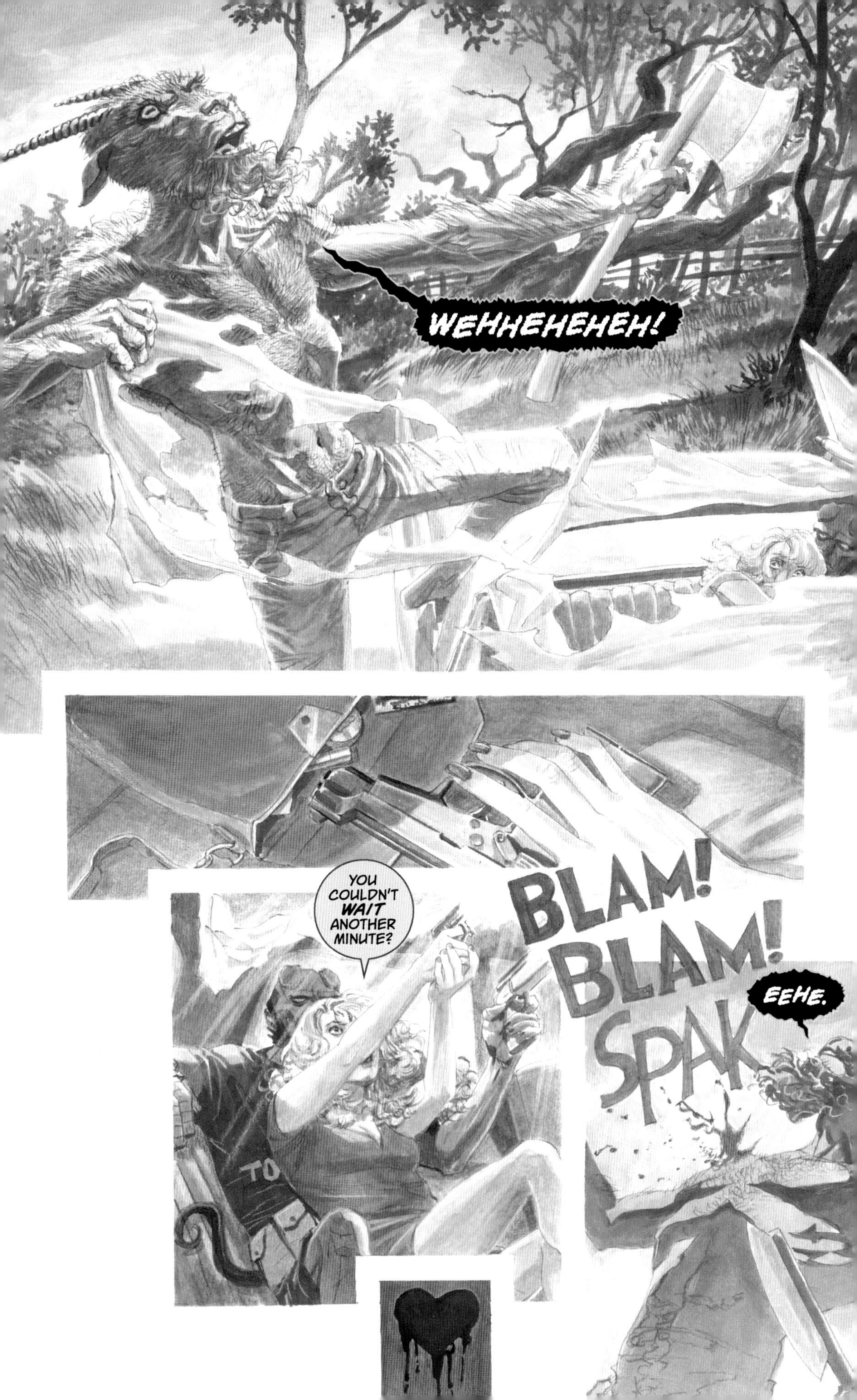

WEHHEHEHEH!
YOU COULDN'T WAIT ANOTHER MINUTE?
BLAM! BLAM!
SPAK
EEHE.

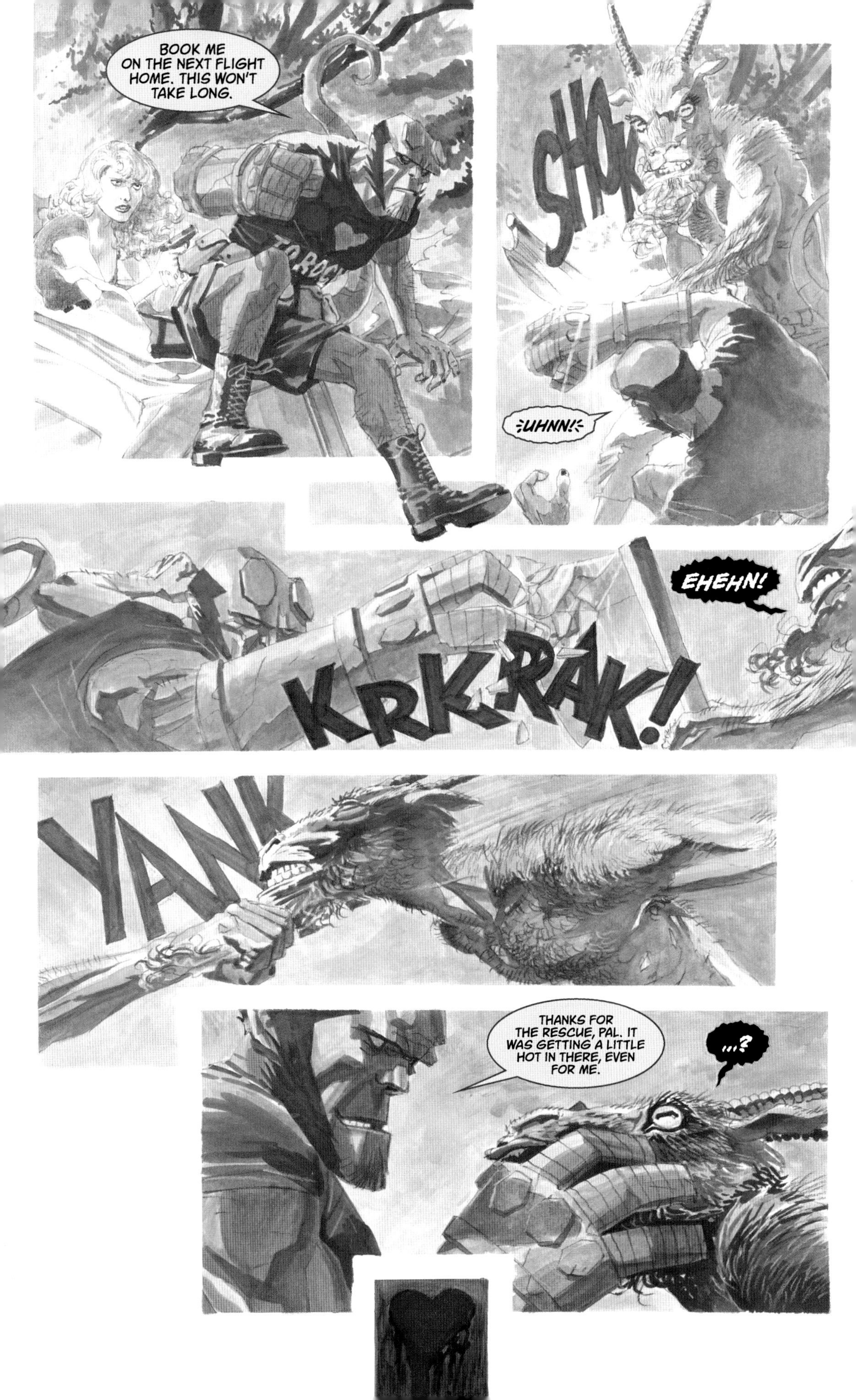
BOOK ME ON THE NEXT FLIGHT HOME. THIS WON'T TAKE LONG.
SHOK
UHNN!
EHEHN!
KRK-RAK!
YANK
THANKS FOR THE RESCUE, PAL. IT WAS GETTING A LITTLE HOT IN THERE, EVEN FOR ME.
...?

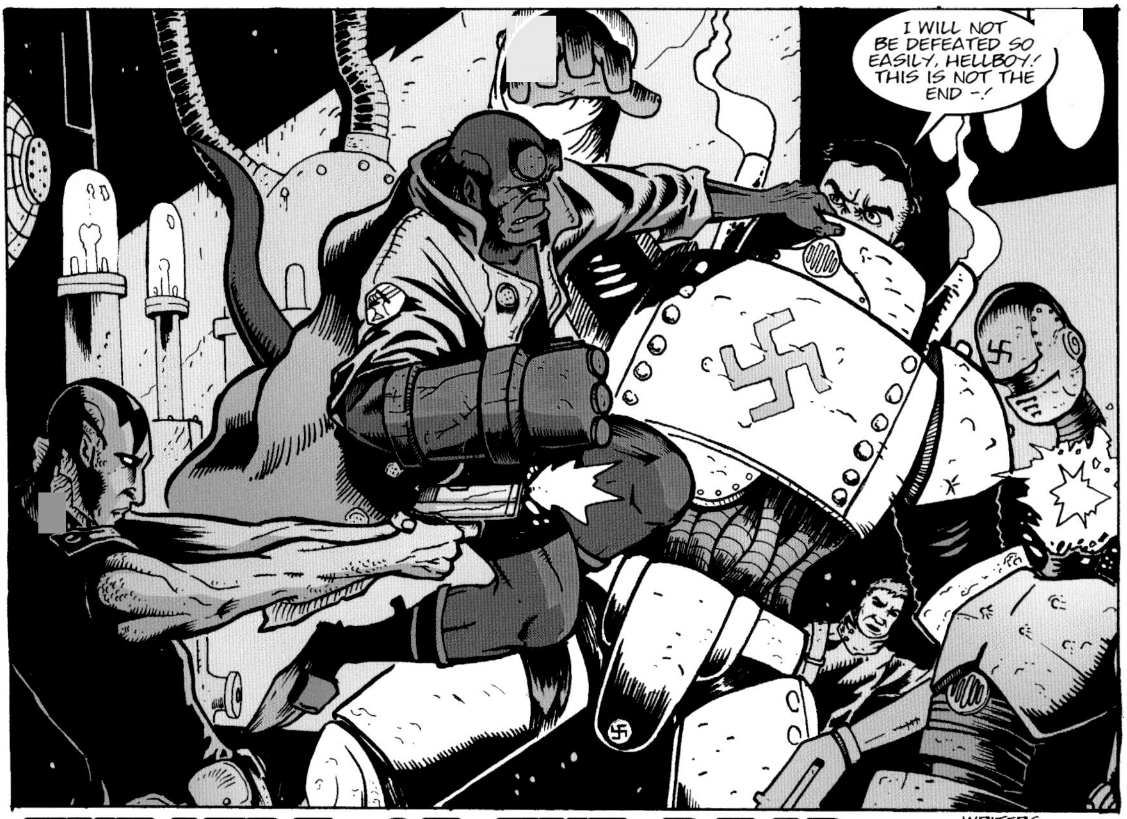
I WILL NOT BE DEFEATED SO EASILY, HELLBOY! THIS IS NOT THE END -!

THEATRE OF THE DEAD

WRITERS-
FASSBENDER AND PASCOE
ARTIST- SIMEON WILKINS
COLORIST- DAVID SELF
LETTERER-
ANNIE PARKHOUSE

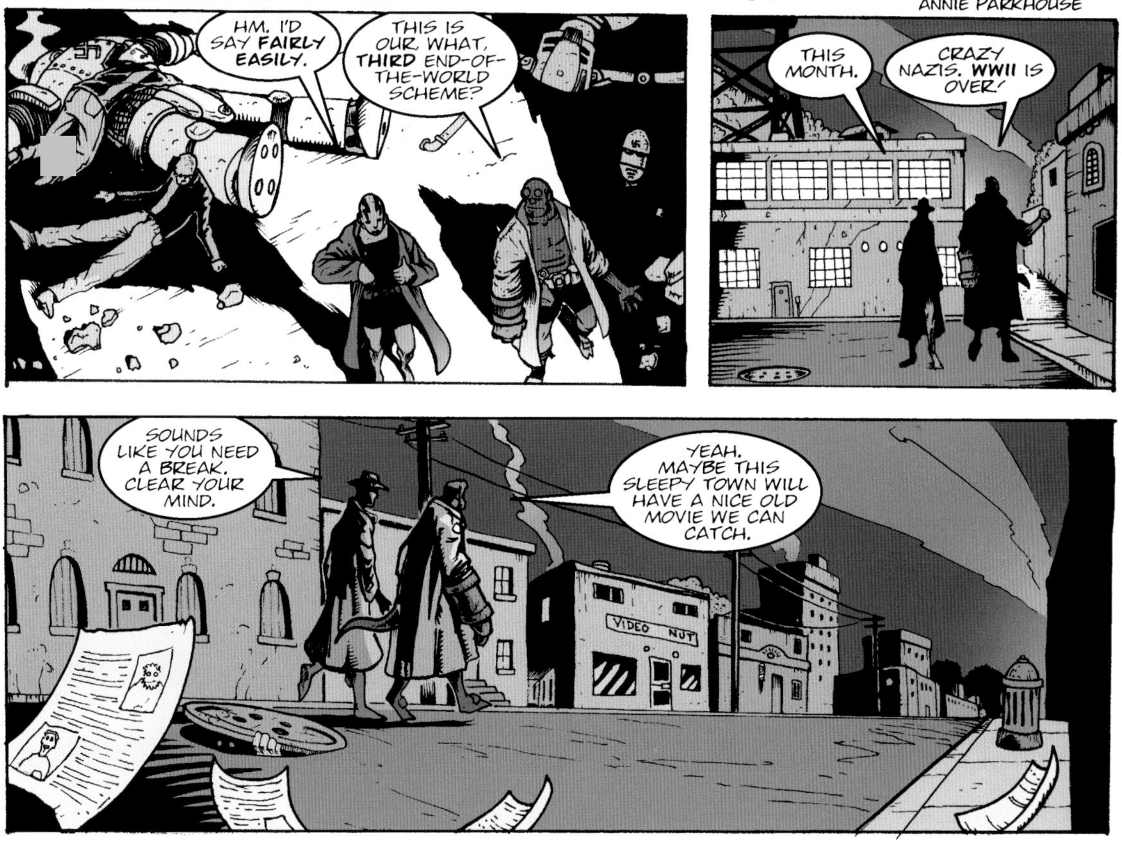
HM. I'D SAY **FAIRLY EASILY**.
THIS IS OUR, WHAT, **THIRD** END-OF-THE-WORLD SCHEME?
THIS MONTH.
CRAZY NAZIS. **WWII** IS OVER!
SOUNDS LIKE YOU NEED A BREAK. CLEAR YOUR MIND.
YEAH. MAYBE THIS SLEEPY TOWN WILL HAVE A NICE OLD MOVIE WE CAN CATCH.
VIDEO NUT

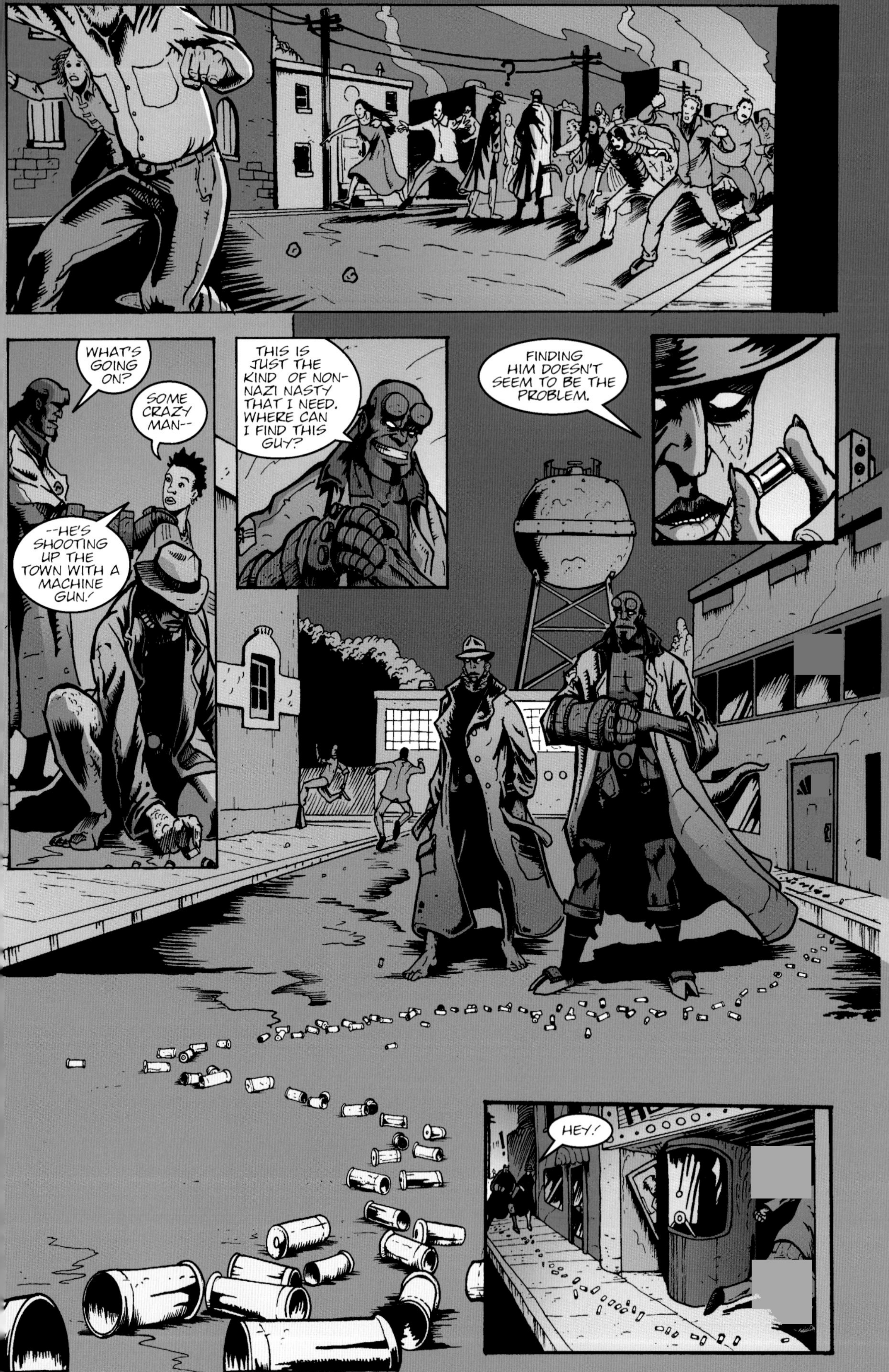
WHAT'S GOING ON?
SOME CRAZY MAN--
--HE'S SHOOTING UP THE TOWN WITH A MACHINE GUN!
THIS IS JUST THE KIND OF NON-NAZI NASTY THAT I NEED. WHERE CAN I FIND THIS GUY?
FINDING HIM DOESN'T SEEM TO BE THE PROBLEM.
HEY!

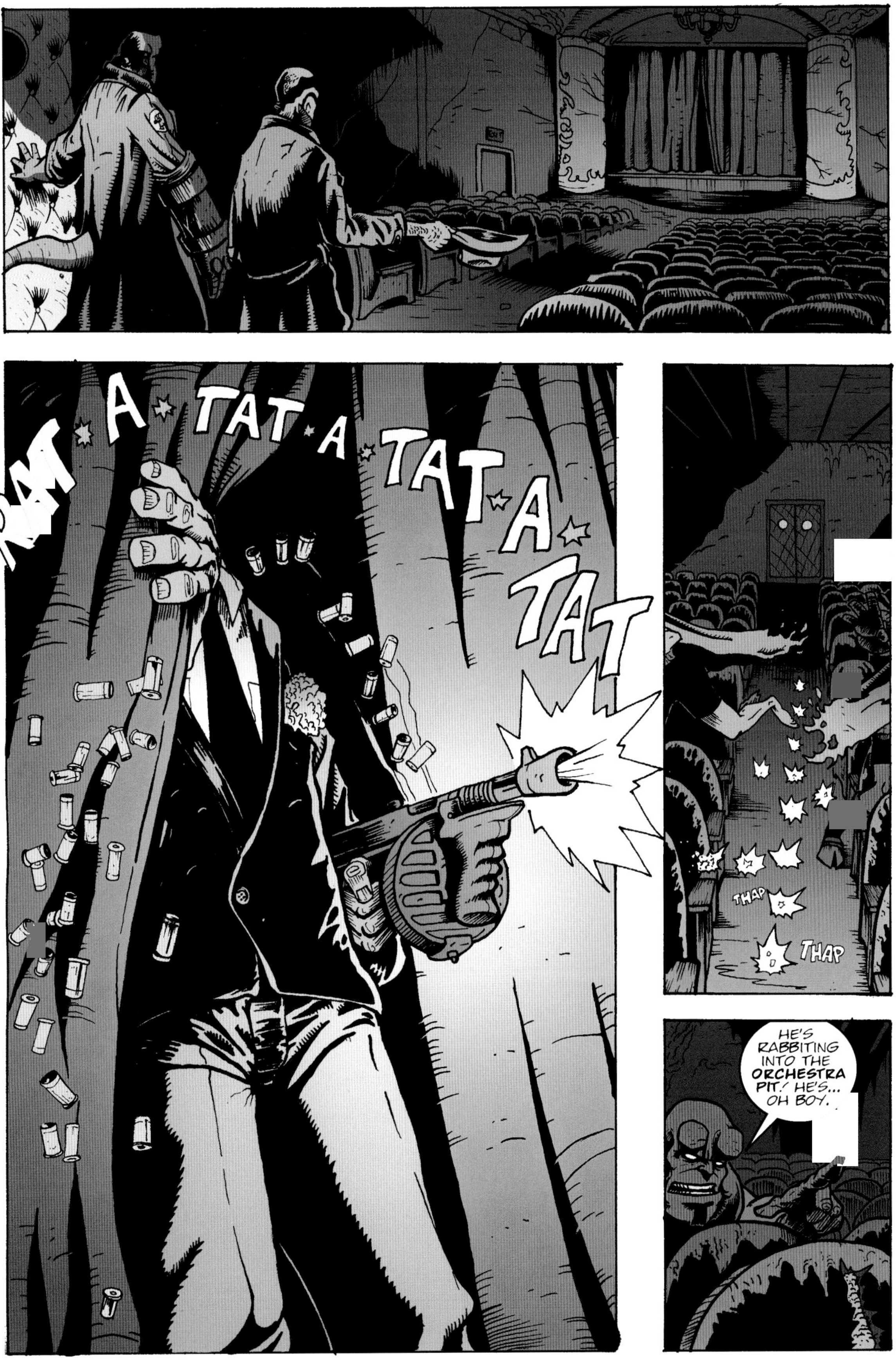
RAT-A-TAT-A-TAT-A-TAT
THAP
THAP
HE'S RABBITING INTO THE ORCHESTRA PIT! HE'S... OH BOY.

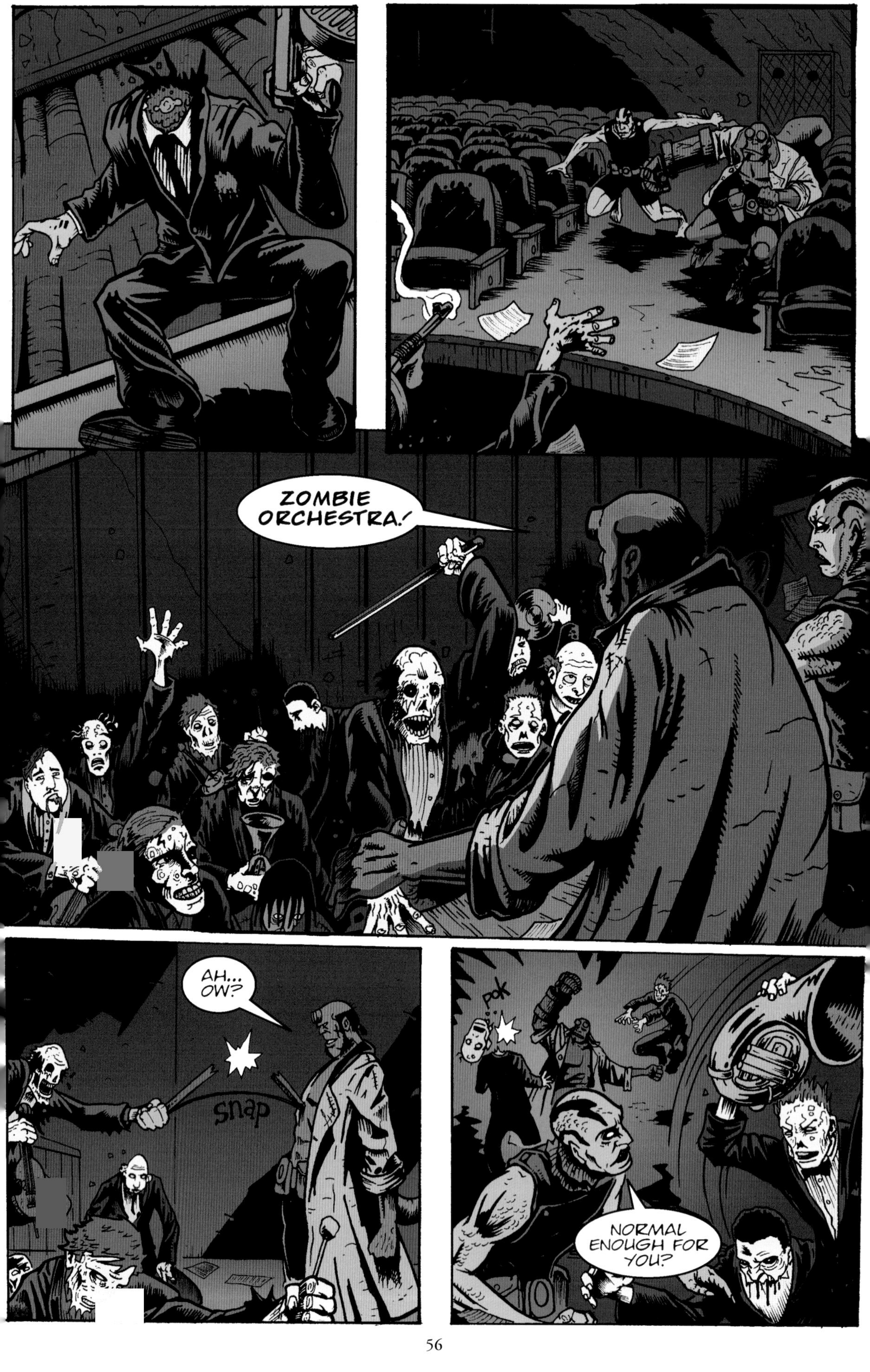
ZOMBIE ORCHESTRA!
AH... OW?
snap
POK
NORMAL ENOUGH FOR YOU?

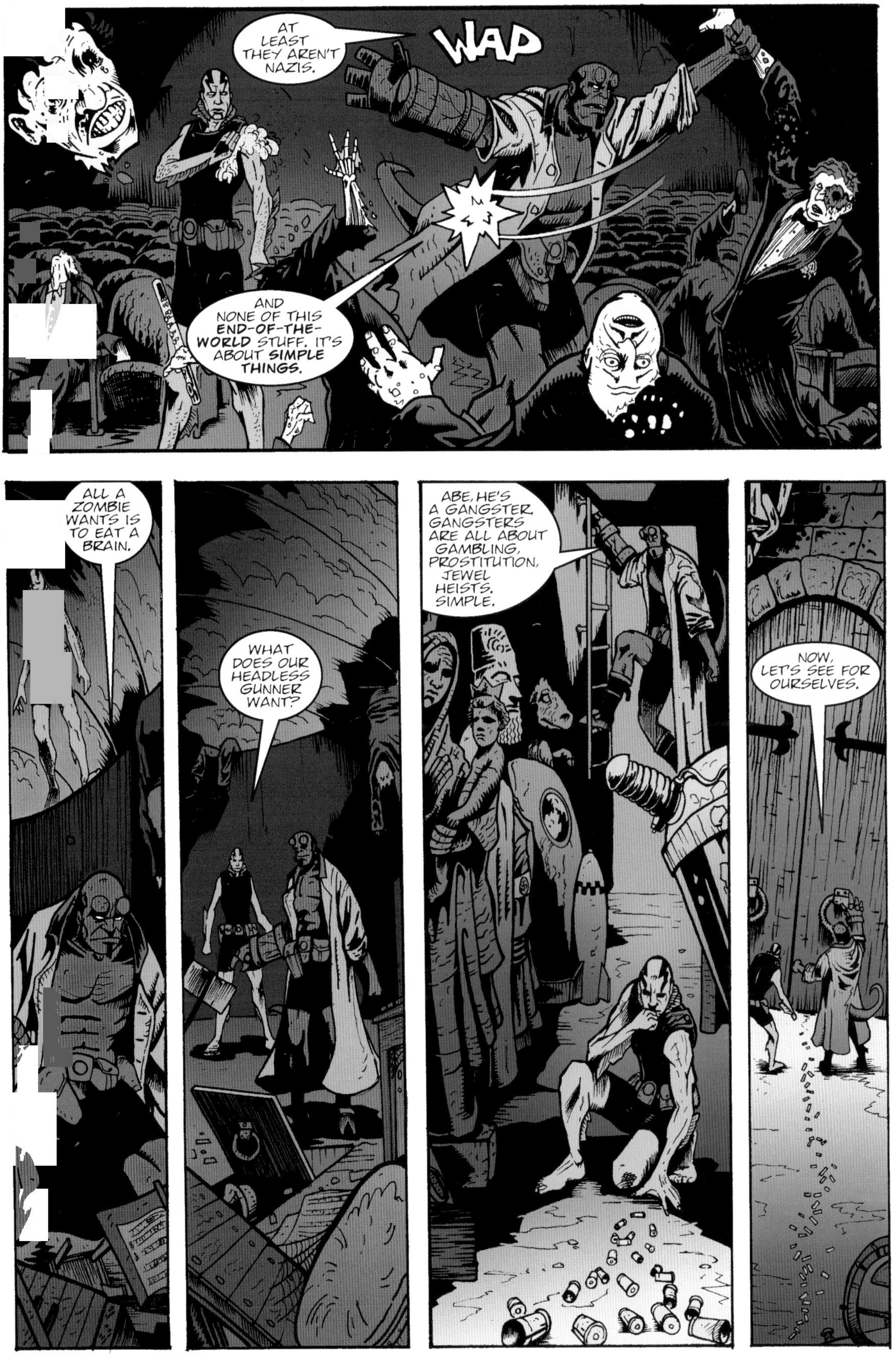
AT LEAST THEY AREN'T NAZIS.
WAP
AND NONE OF THIS END-OF-THE-WORLD STUFF. IT'S ABOUT SIMPLE THINGS.
ALL A ZOMBIE WANTS IS TO EAT A BRAIN.
WHAT DOES OUR HEADLESS GUNNER WANT?
ABE, HE'S A GANGSTER. GANGSTERS ARE ALL ABOUT GAMBLING, PROSTITUTION, JEWEL HEISTS. SIMPLE.
NOW, LET'S SEE FOR OURSELVES.

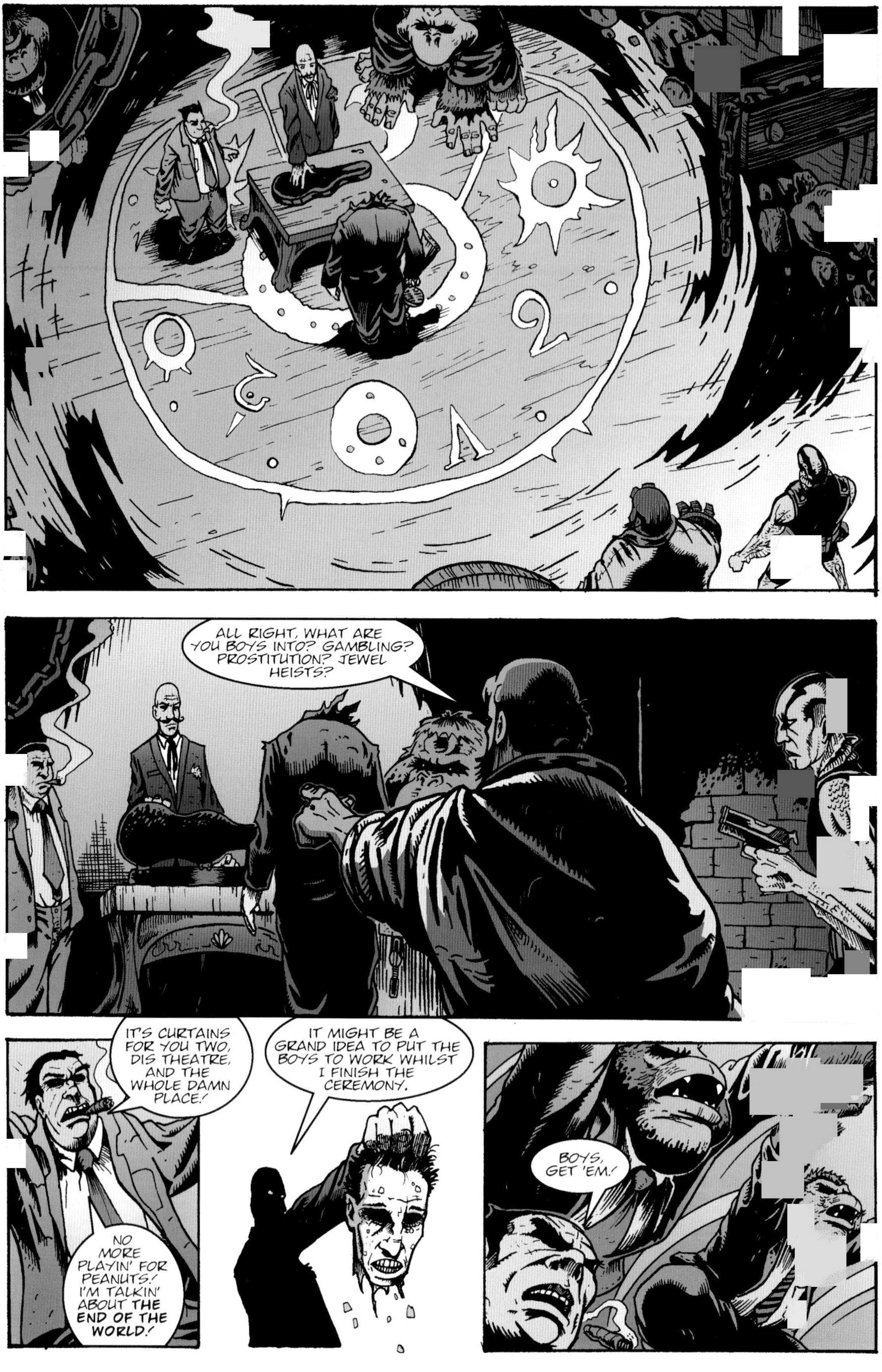

ALL RIGHT, WHAT ARE YOU BOYS INTO? GAMBLING? PROSTITUTION? JEWEL HEISTS?
IT'S CURTAINS FOR YOU TWO, DIS THEATRE, AND THE WHOLE DAMN PLACE!
NO MORE PLAYIN' FOR PEANUTS! I'M TALKIN' ABOUT THE END OF THE WORLD!
IT MIGHT BE A GRAND IDEA TO PUT THE BOYS TO WORK WHILST I FINISH THE CEREMONY.
BOYS, GET 'EM!

Spak

BLAM

YA IGNORAMUS! DAT HEAD IS THE KEY!

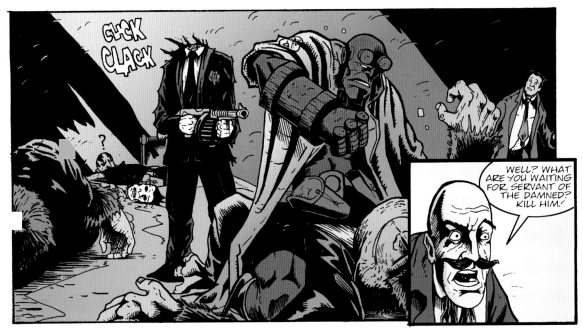

CLICK CLACK

?

WELL? WHAT ARE YOU WAITING FOR, SERVANT OF THE DAMNED? KILL HIM!

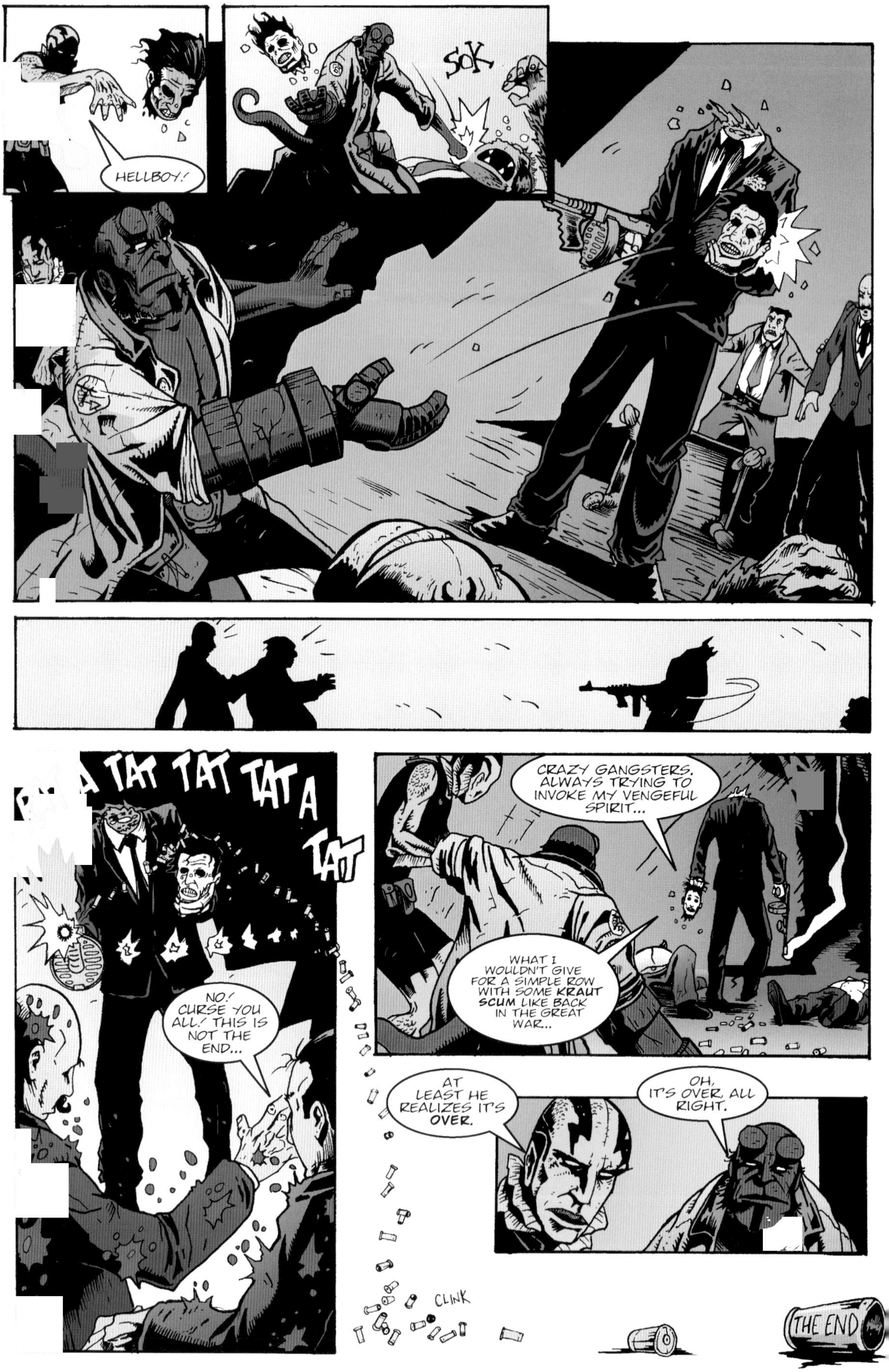
HELLBOY!
SOK
TAT TAT TATA TAT
NO! CURSE YOU ALL! THIS IS NOT THE END...
CRAZY GANGSTERS. ALWAYS TRYING TO INVOKE MY VENGEFUL SPIRIT...
WHAT I WOULDN'T GIVE FOR A SIMPLE ROW WITH SOME KRAUT SCUM LIKE BACK IN THE GREAT WAR...
AT LEAST HE REALIZES IT'S OVER.
OH, IT'S OVER, ALL RIGHT.
CLINK
THE END

SASAKI-SAN!

I HAVEN'T SEEN YOU SINCE THE KAPPA KIDNAPPING IN KOBE.

HOW THE HECK--?

IT IS A PLEASURE TO SEE YOU AGAIN AS WELL, HELLBOY-SAN.

SO WHAT'S THE SCORE HERE?

INTERESTING CHOICE OF WORDS, AS IT IS INDEED GHOSTLY GAMES WE MAY END UP PLAYING THIS NIGHT.

THIS IS A UNIQUE CASE. THESE ARE THE SPIRITS OF CHILDREN, HELLBOY-SAN. RESTLESS SPIRITS WHO DIED FAR TOO YOUNG, BEFORE EXPERIENCING MUCH JOY IN THEIR LIVES.

THESE GUYS SAY THEIR WAREHOUSE IS HAUNTED BY GHOSTS--BUT SPIRITS PLAYING WITH DOLLS? WHAT GOOD DOES THAT DO THEM?

THEY ARE SEEKING THE FUN THEY WERE DENIED WHEN THEIR LIVES WERE CUT SHORT.

KIDS.

WONDERFUL.

THERE'S NOTHING WORSE THAN IMMATURE APPARITIONS.

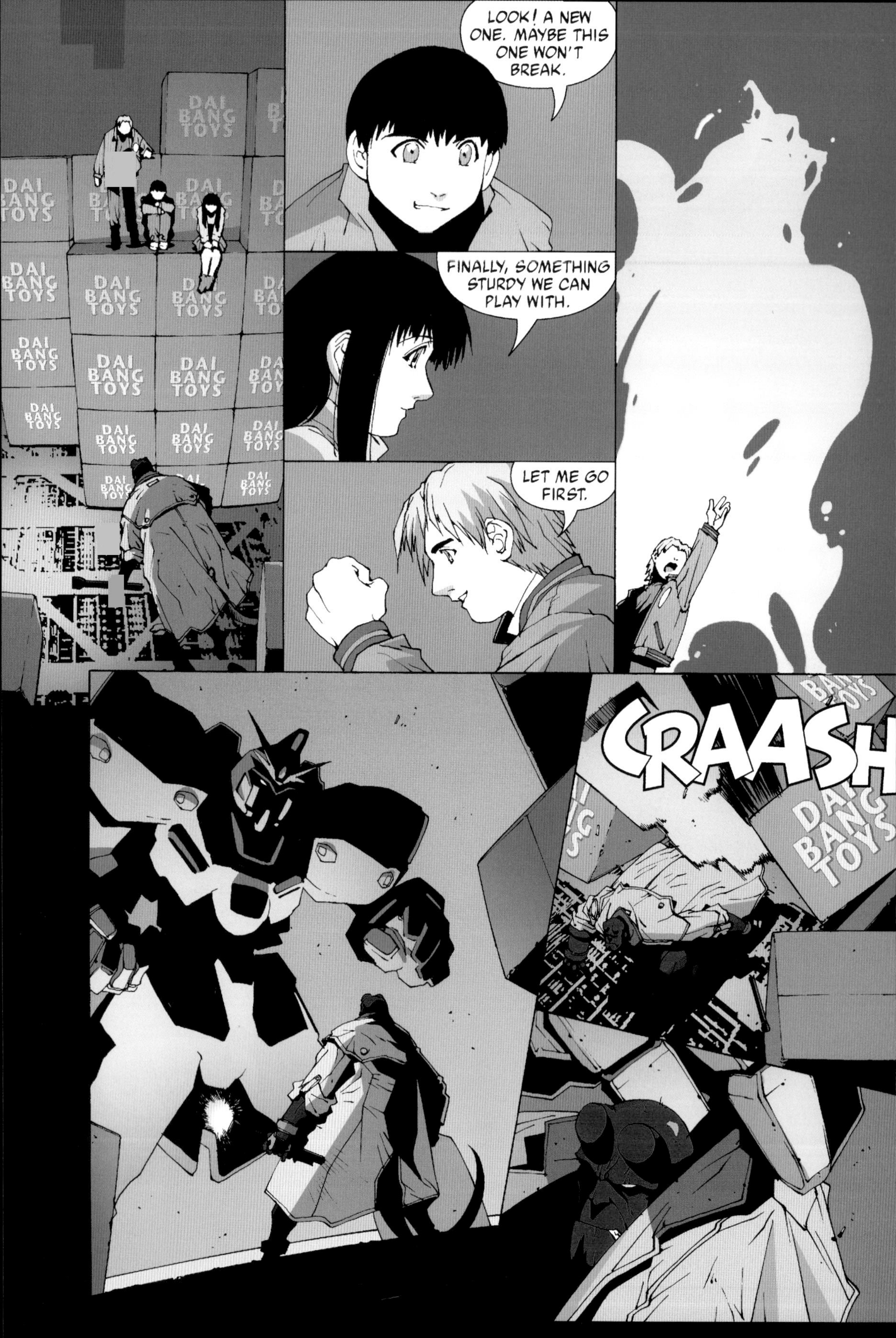

DAI BANG TOYS
LOOK! A NEW ONE. MAYBE THIS ONE WON'T BREAK.
FINALLY, SOMETHING STURDY WE CAN PLAY WITH.
LET ME GO FIRST.
CRAASH
DAI BANG TOYS

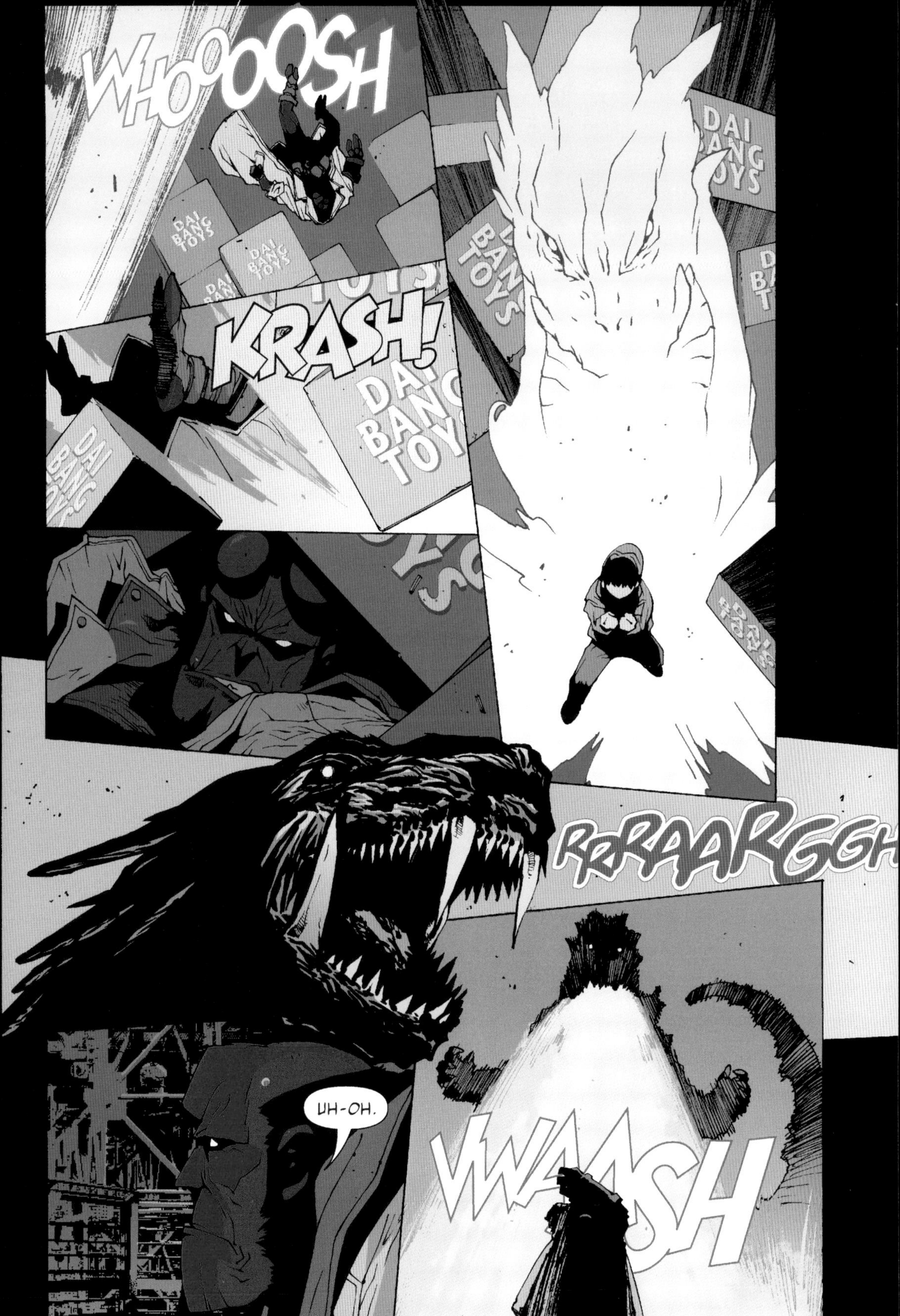
WHOOOOSH
DAI BANG TOYS
KRASH!
RRRAARGGH
UH-OH.
VWAASH

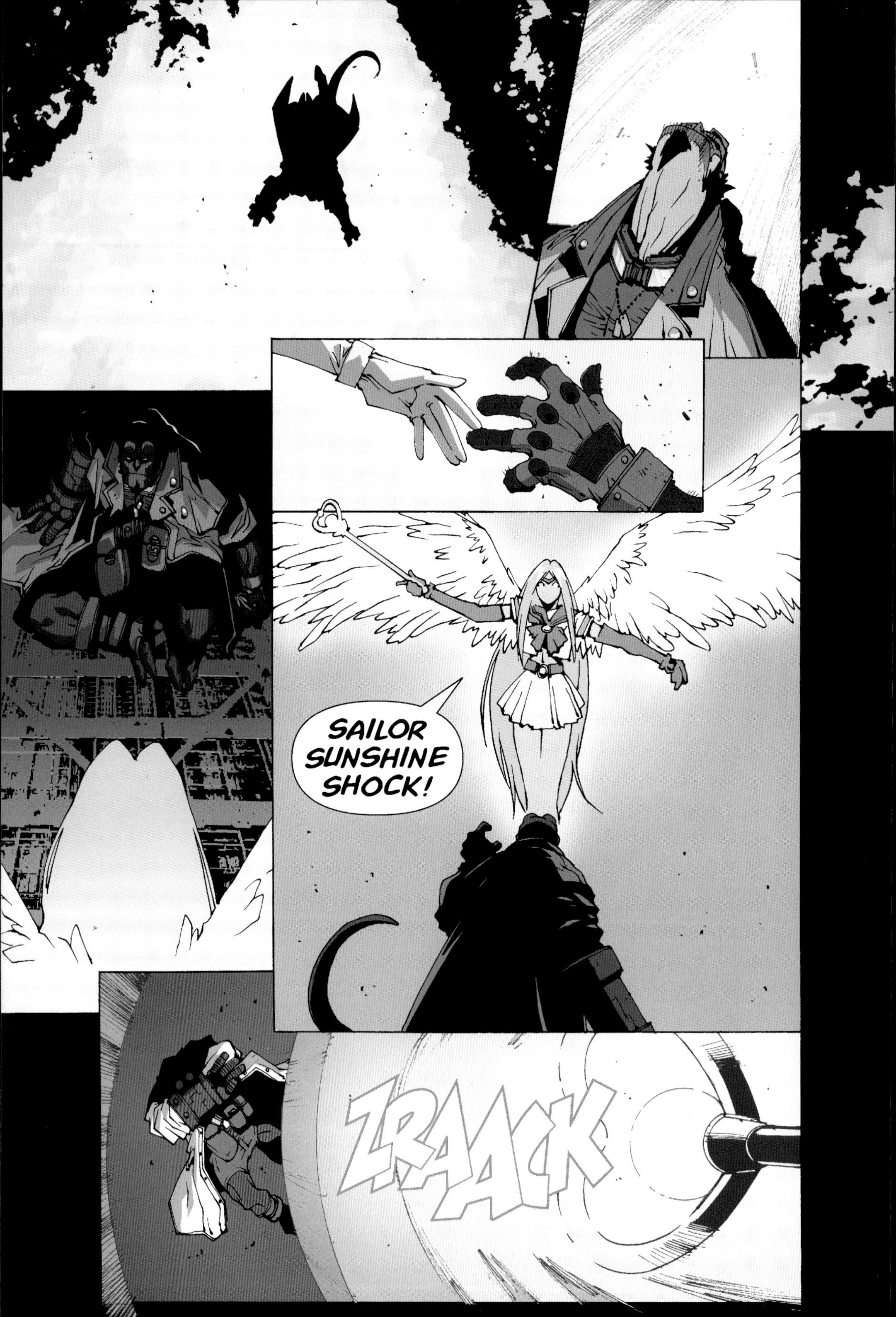
SAILOR SUNSHINE SHOCK!
ZRAACK

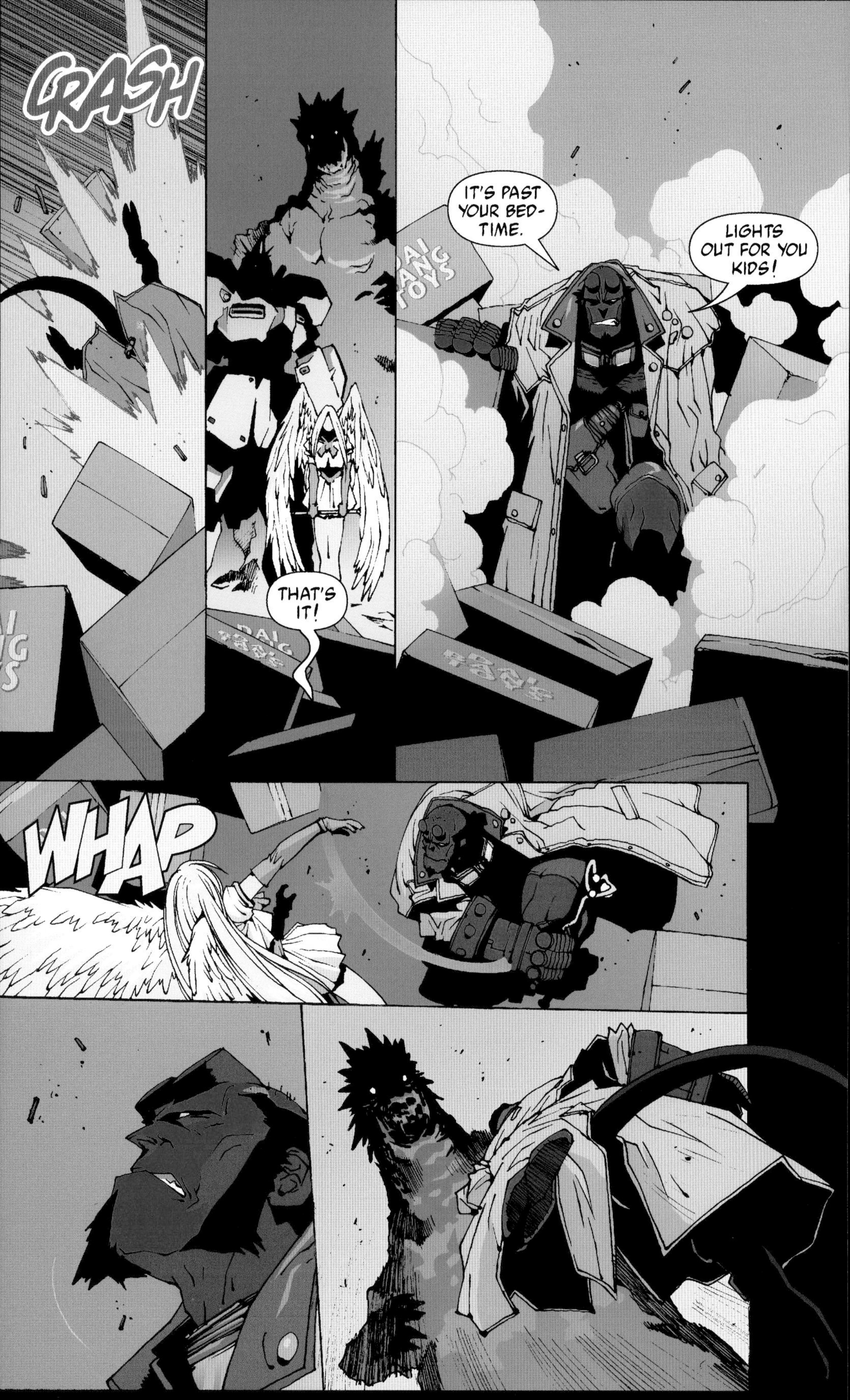
CRASH
IT'S PAST YOUR BED-TIME.
LIGHTS OUT FOR YOU KIDS!
THAT'S IT!
WHAP

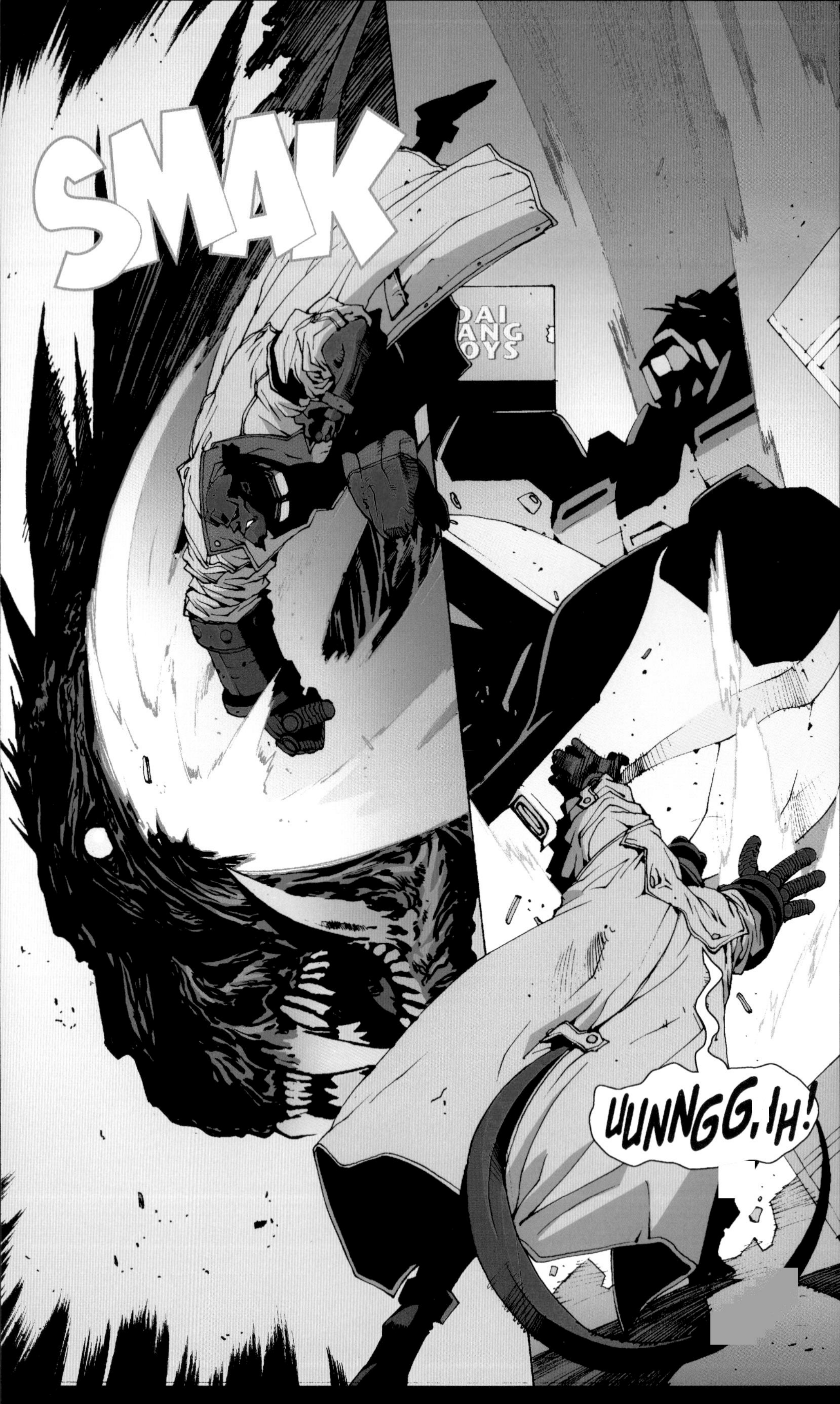
SMAK
DAI
ANG
OYS
UUNNGG, IH!

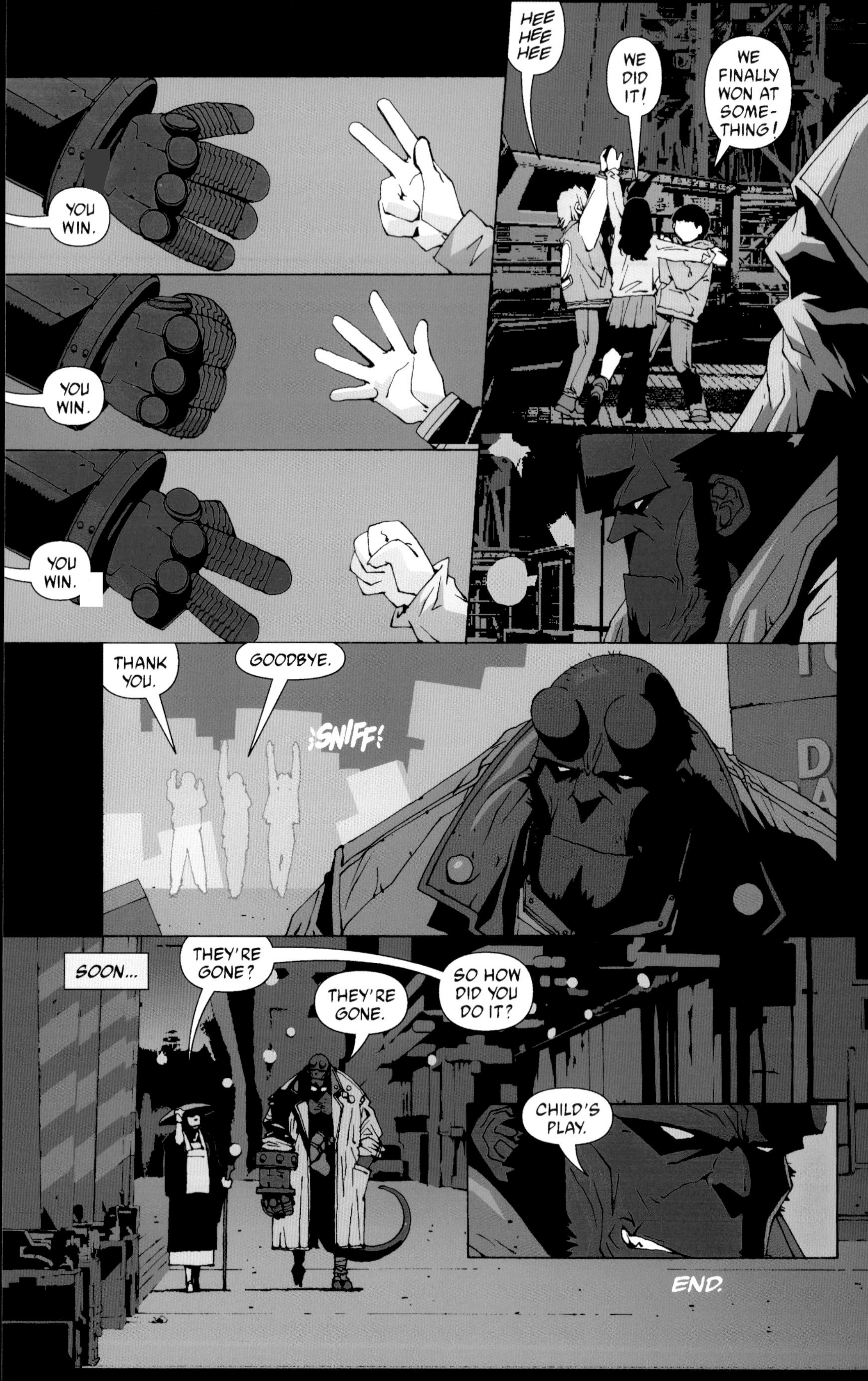
YOU WIN.
YOU WIN.
YOU WIN.
HEE HEE HEE
WE DID IT!
WE FINALLY WON AT SOME-THING!
THANK YOU.
GOODBYE.
SNIFF
SOON...
THEY'RE GONE?
THEY'RE GONE.
SO HOW DID YOU DO IT?
CHILD'S PLAY.
END.

"WE WERE SENT TO INVESTIGATE A CHURCH BURNING SIMILAR TO THE MID-'90s ARSONS SET BY THE NEO-PAGAN, NATIONALIST BLACK METAL UNDERGROUND."

"WHAT SET THIS CASE APART WAS THE **BODY** FOUND IN THE RUINS."

"THE CAUSE OF DEATH WASN'T FIRE, BUT AN UNDETERMINED ACIDIC SUBSTANCE."

"THE GIRL WAS IDENTIFIED AS A FOLLOWER OF THE NORWEIGAN BAND **OSKOREI**, WHO HAD FORMED A NEW BLACK METAL MOVEMENT CALLED THE **BARFROST ORDEN**."

"OSKOREI'S LEADER WAS ONE **DIDRIK BILLERBECK**, AKA **MORTHVARGR**, AKA "THE **CHIEFTAN**". MONTHS EARLIER, HE AND HIS BAND HAD SET OFF FOR THE JOTUNHEIM MOUNTAINS TO BE CLOSER TO NATURE AND THE OLD GODS."

osforei

BILLERBECK

TEL: 0557.

"NO ONE HAD SEEN THEM SINCE."

"IZZY COULDN'T GET ANYTHING ON DIDRIK OR THE GIRL FROM THE LOCAL METAL KIDS."

"BUT HE **DID** PICK UP THE LOCATION OF A SECRET GATHERING OF THE TRIBES."

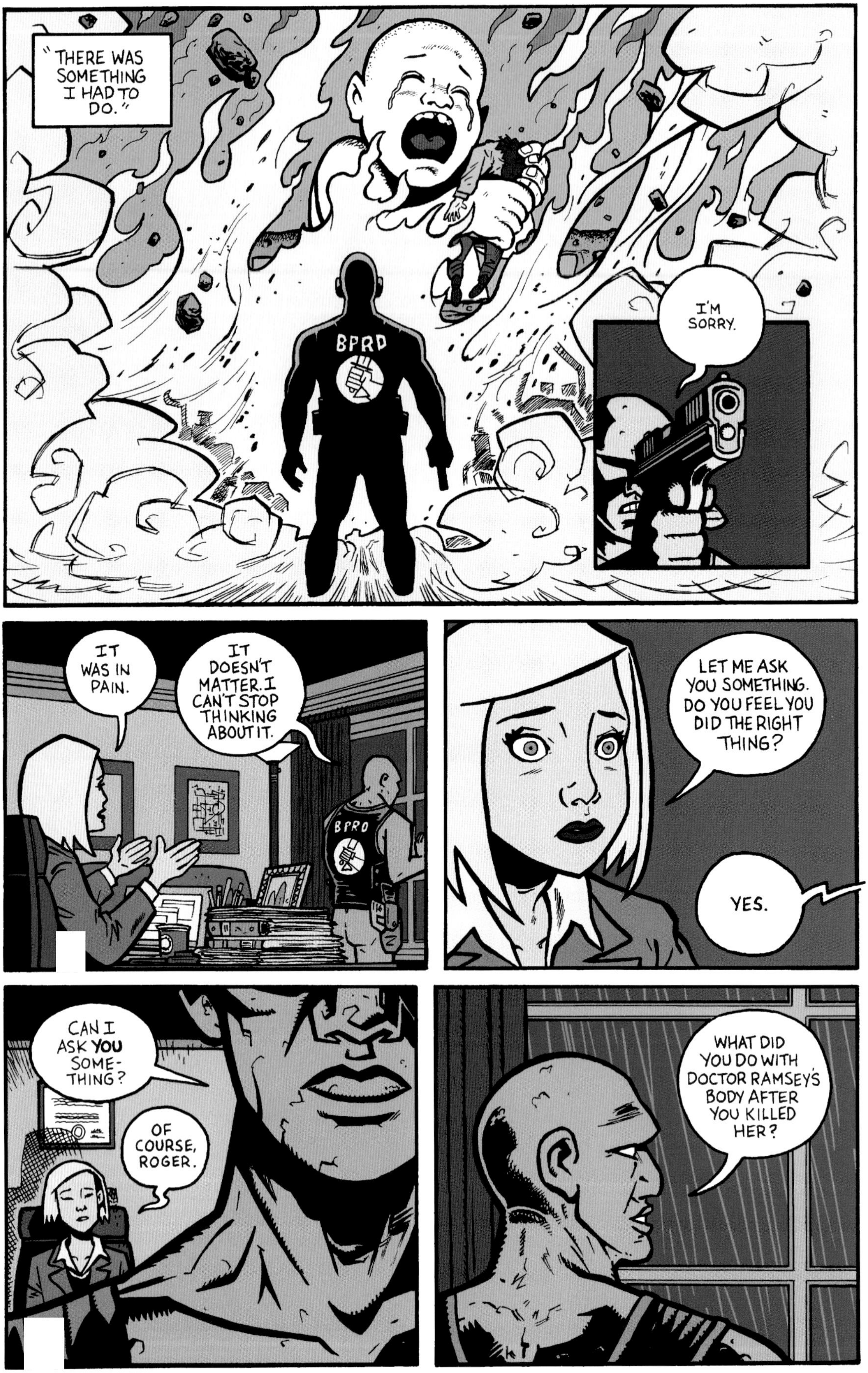
"THERE WAS SOMETHING I HAD TO DO."
BPRD
I'M SORRY.
IT WAS IN PAIN.
IT DOESN'T MATTER. I CAN'T STOP THINKING ABOUT IT.
BPRD
LET ME ASK YOU SOMETHING. DO YOU FEEL YOU DID THE RIGHT THING?
YES.
CAN I ASK YOU SOMETHING?
OF COURSE, ROGER.
WHAT DID YOU DO WITH DOCTOR RAMSEY'S BODY AFTER YOU KILLED HER?

SHE'S BURIED OUT BACK, WITH HER DOG.

SINCE OFFICER D'AMICO'S SUICIDE. YOUR FORMER PATIENT -- OR VICTIM -- HAD FRIENDS IN HIGH PLACES.

WE FOUND LESIONS IN HIS BRAIN CAUSED BY PSYCHIC VAMPIRISM. WE SUSPECTED A TEMHOT. A GRIEF EATER.

AND HERE YOU ARE.

HOW LONG HAVE YOU KNOWN?

WHAT WOULD YOU HAVE DONE IF I HADN'T REVEALED MYSELF?

THROWN SALT IN YOUR EYES, TO SEE IF YOU CRIED BLOOD.

HMM. YOUR MASTERS TAUGHT YOU WELL, HOMUNCULUS.

RAKK

BUT NOT WELL ENOUGH.

STUPIDER STILL. YOUR GUN IS USE-LESS HERE.

THAT'S WHY I BROUGHT THIS.

BLACK AND DECKER CORDLESS, RIGGED WITH NAILS FROM YOUR VICTIM'S COFFIN--

K-CHUNT

PROFESSIONAL HELP • EVAN DORKIN (SCRIPT/ART) • SARAH DYER (COLORS/DIALOGUE ASSIST)

THE END

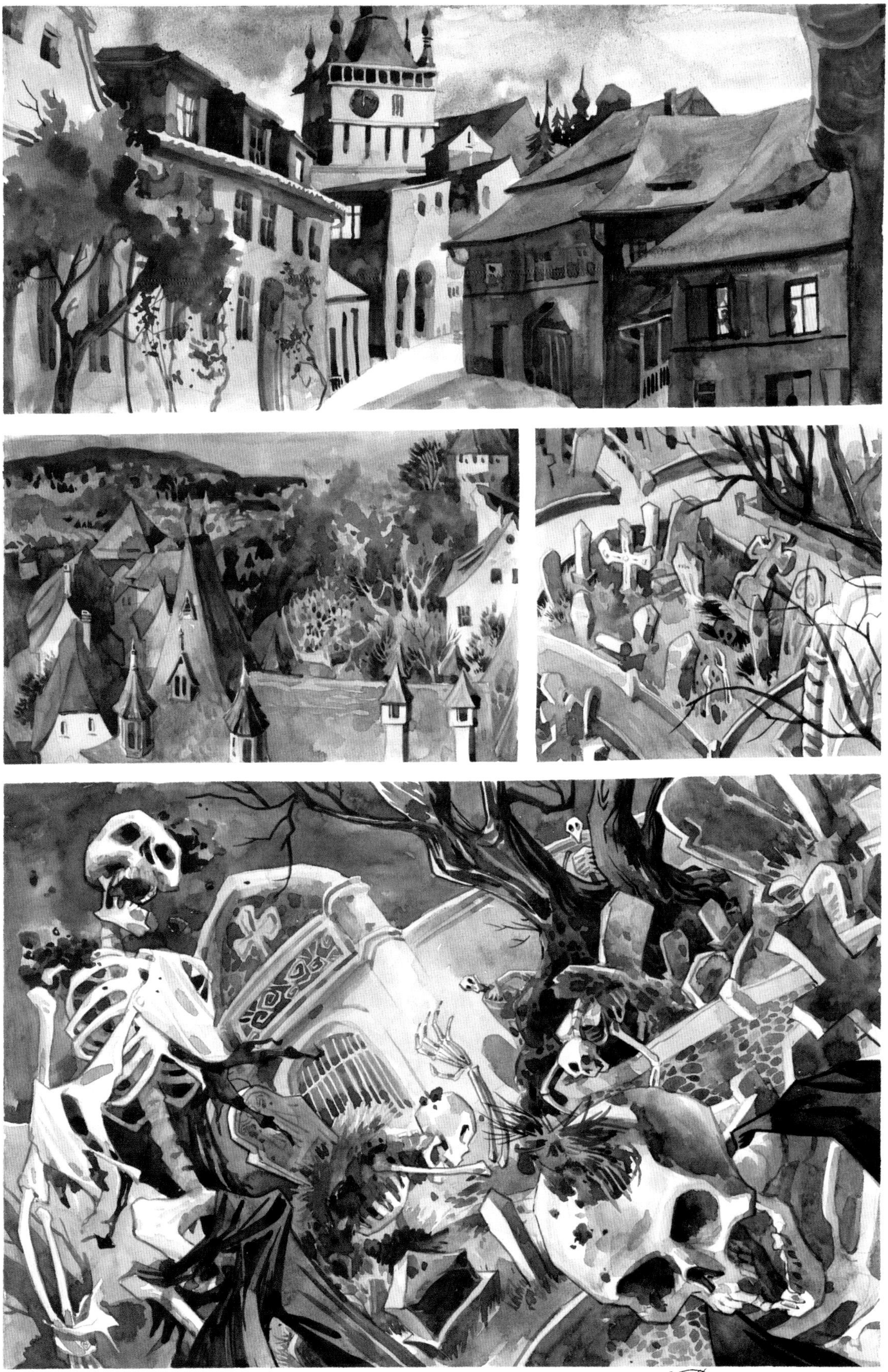

Fifteen Minutes... 2004

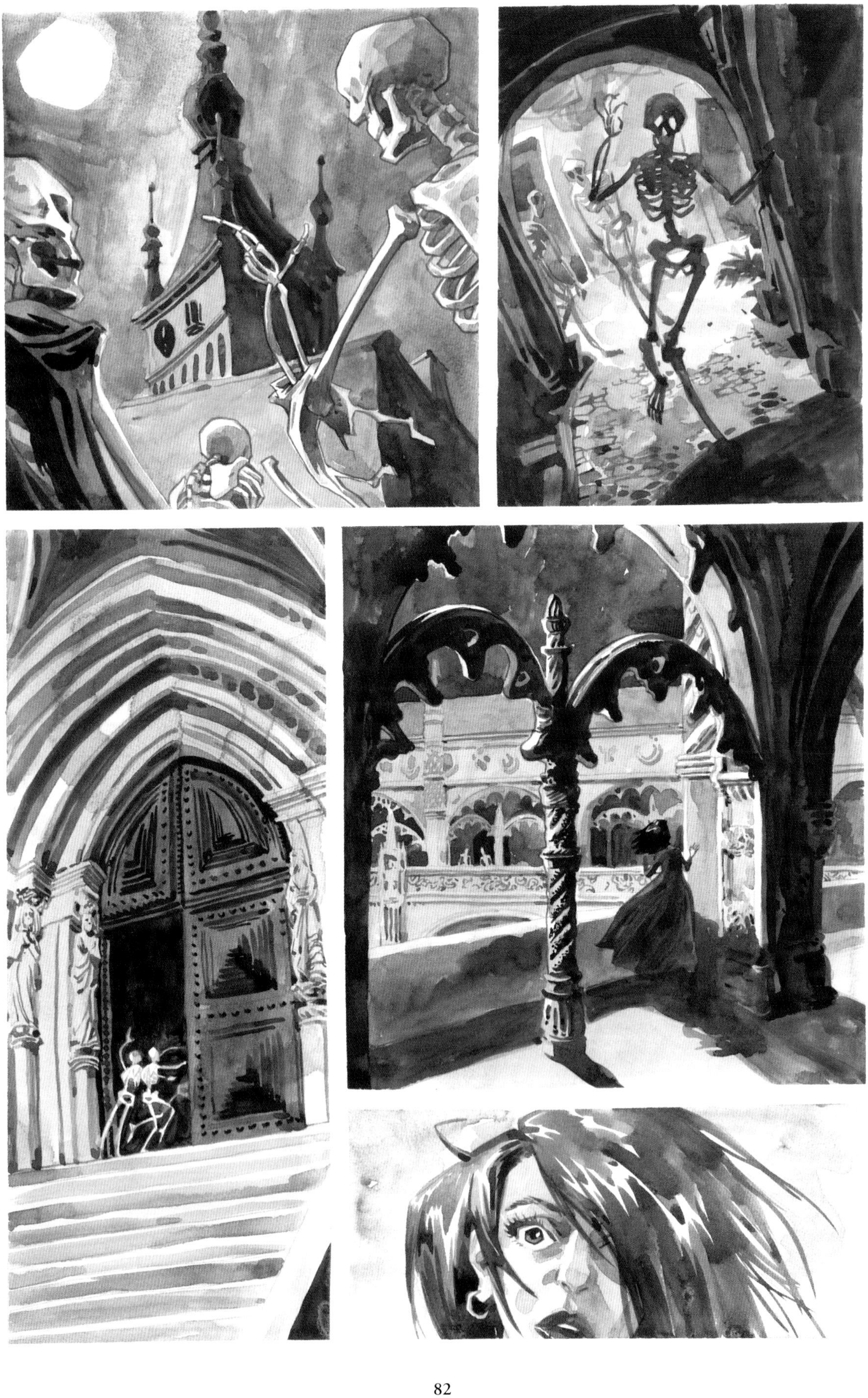

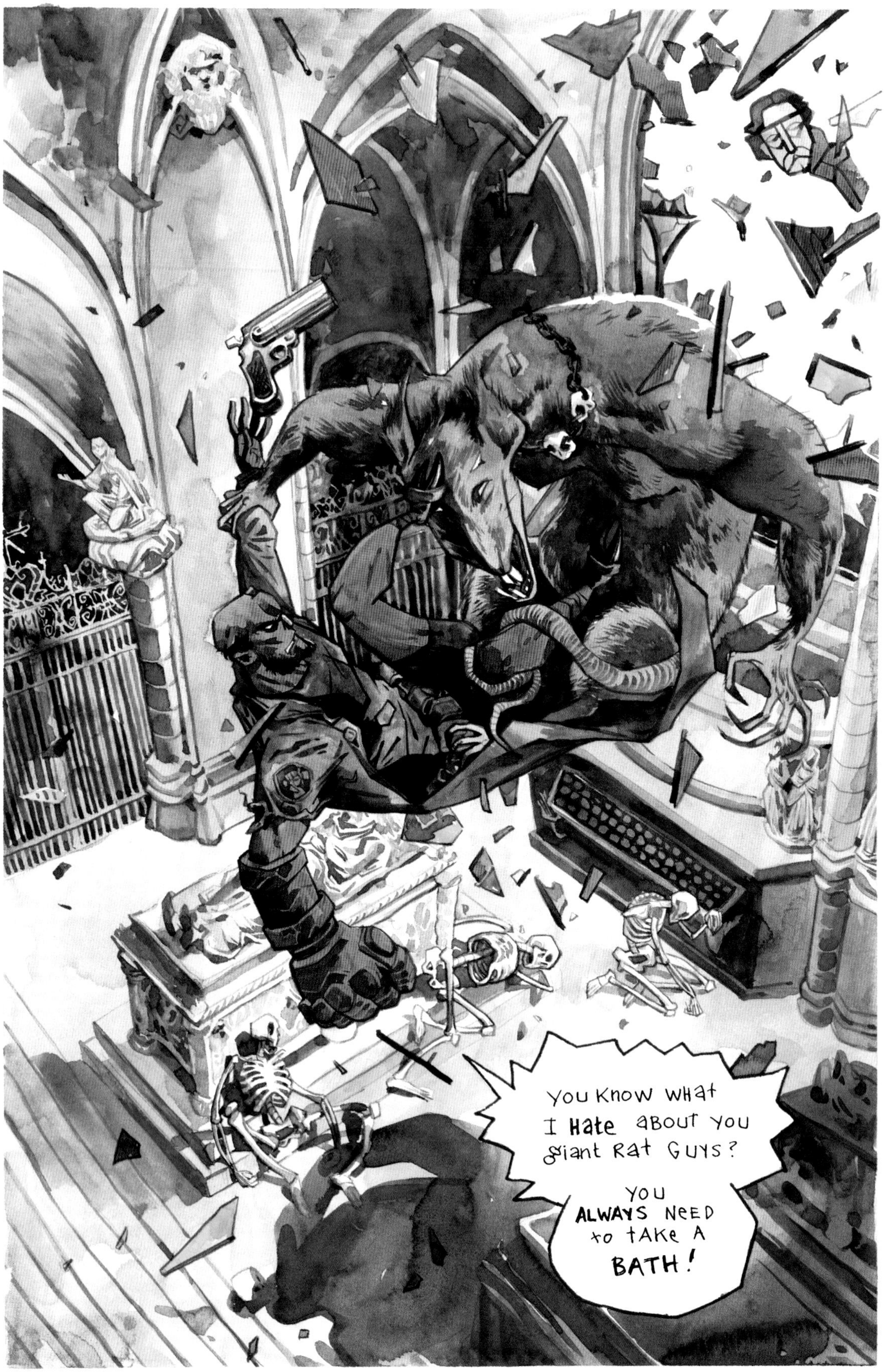
YOU KNOW WHAT I HATE ABOUT YOU GIANT RAT GUYS?
YOU ALWAYS NEED TO TAKE A BATH!

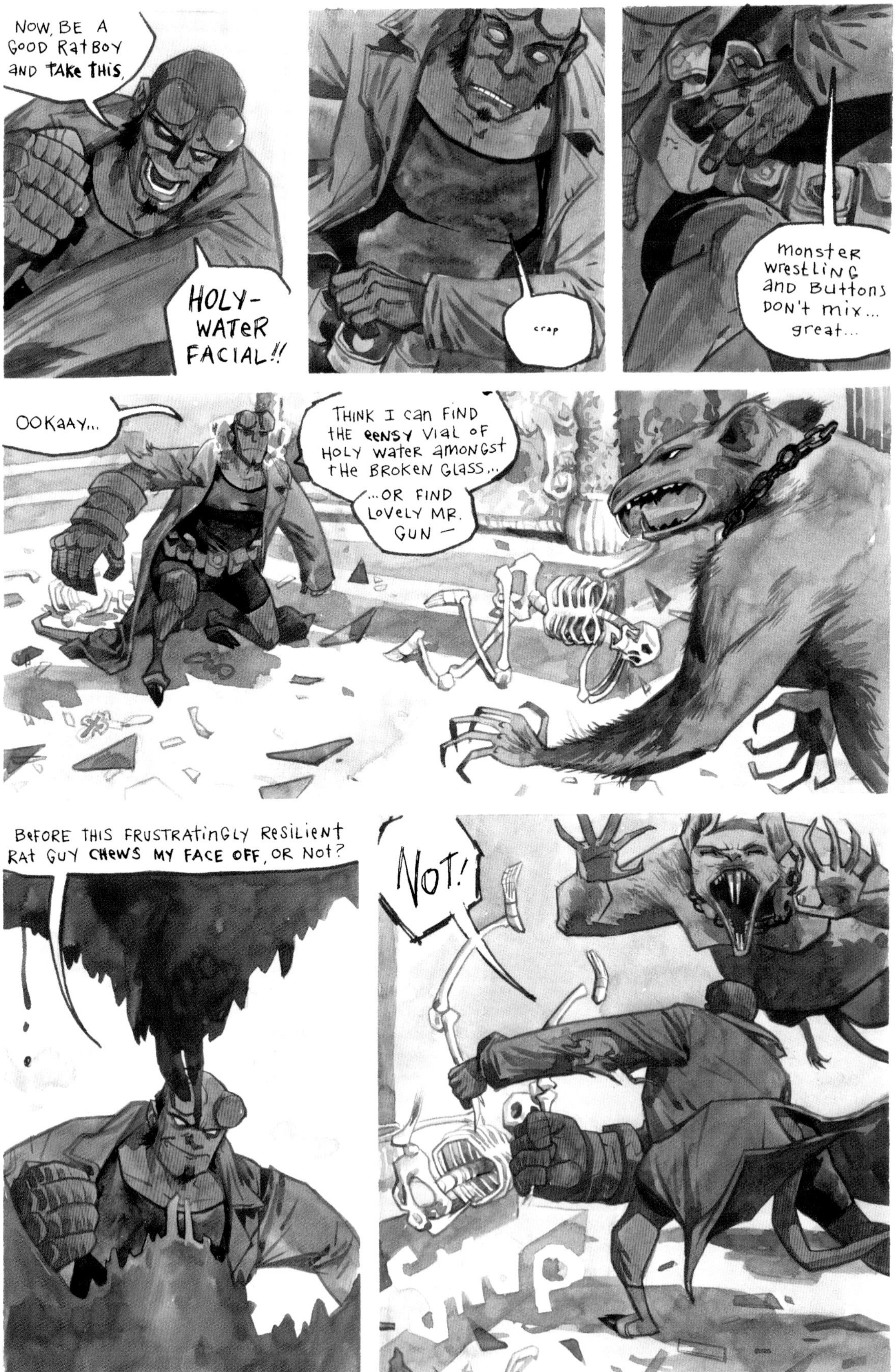
NOW, BE A GOOD RatBOY AND TAKE THIS,
HOLY-WATER FACIAL!!
crap
monster wrestling and Buttons DON'T mix... great...
OOKaAY...
THINK I can FIND the eensy vial of HOLY water amongst the BROKEN GLASS...
...OR FIND LOVELY MR. GUN —
BEFORE THIS FRUSTRATINGLY RESILIENT RAT GUY CHEWS MY FACE OFF, OR NOT?
NOT!

THAT'S WHAT'S GOOD FOR YOU !!

C'MON, STINKY.

man. THAT WAS A nice WINDOW.

WHY Don't I CARRY A HOLY-WATER **PISTOL** ? YEESH...

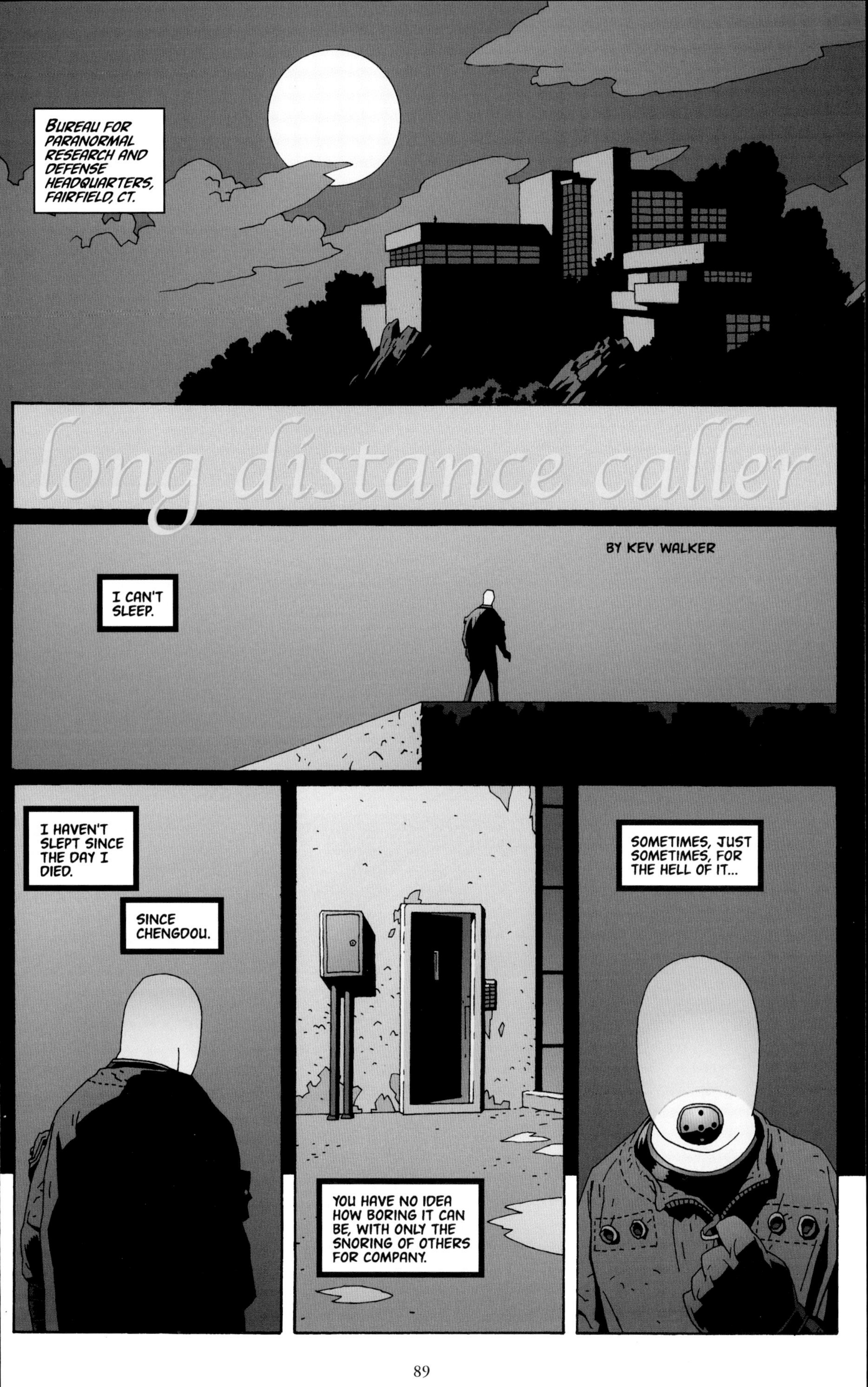
BUREAU FOR PARANORMAL RESEARCH AND DEFENSE HEADQUARTERS, FAIRFIELD, CT.
long distance caller
BY KEV WALKER
I CAN'T SLEEP.
I HAVEN'T SLEPT SINCE THE DAY I DIED.
SINCE CHENGDOU.
YOU HAVE NO IDEA HOW BORING IT CAN BE, WITH ONLY THE SNORING OF OTHERS FOR COMPANY.
SOMETIMES, JUST SOMETIMES, FOR THE HELL OF IT...

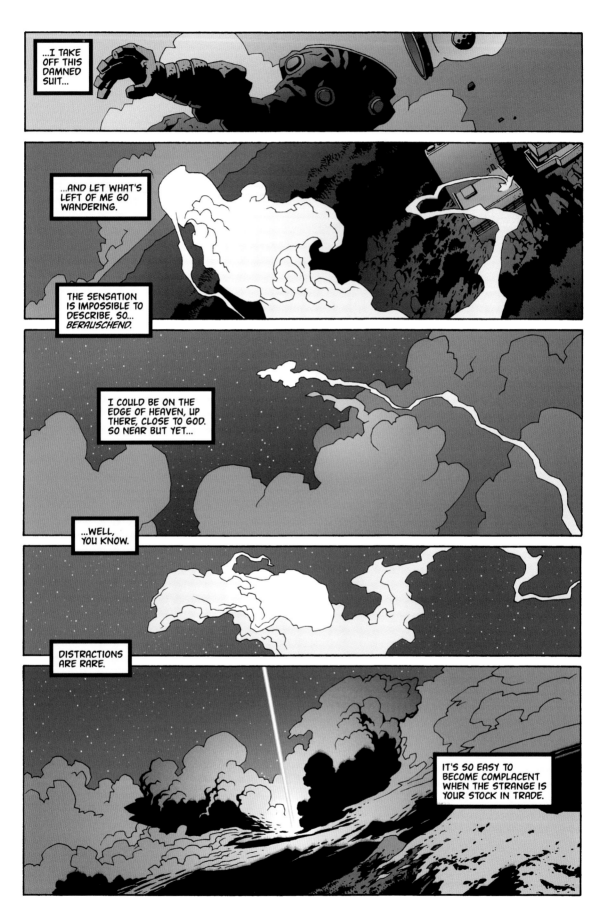

...I TAKE OFF THIS DAMNED SUIT...

...AND LET WHAT'S LEFT OF ME GO WANDERING.

THE SENSATION IS IMPOSSIBLE TO DESCRIBE, SO... *BERAUSCHEND.*

I COULD BE ON THE EDGE OF HEAVEN, UP THERE, CLOSE TO GOD. SO NEAR BUT YET...

...WELL, YOU KNOW.

DISTRACTIONS ARE RARE.

IT'S SO EASY TO BECOME COMPLACENT WHEN THE STRANGE IS YOUR STOCK IN TRADE.

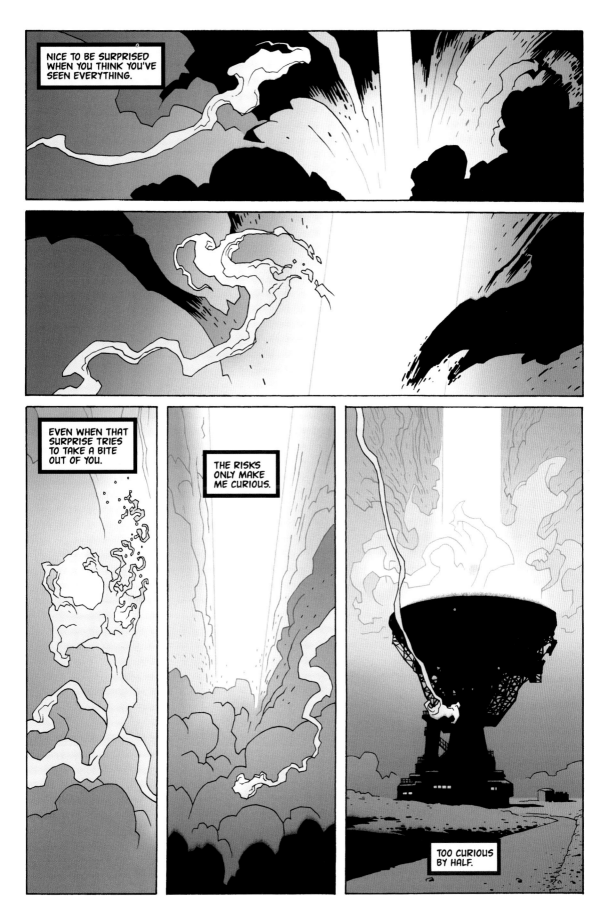

-- BY SOMETHING NOT OF THIS WORLD.

SOMETHING ALIVE...

...BELLIGERENT...

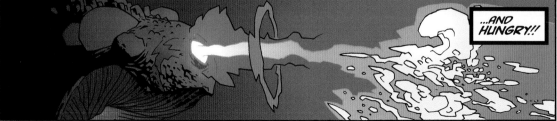

...AND HUNGRY!!

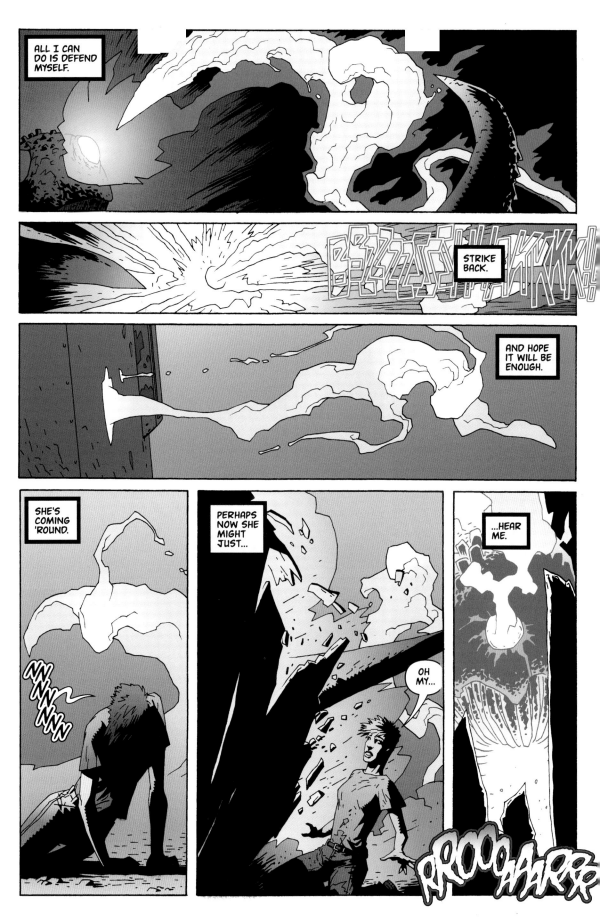

THE POWER, GIRL, KILL THE POWER.

GOT TO KILL THE POWER.

MEIN GOTT, SHE HEARD ME.

WHY THE HELL DID I THINK OF THAT?

RRAAAAR

WRRRMMMMMM

I HOPE THIS IS COVERED ON MY INSURANCE.

VROOOOO!!

*SEARCH FOR EXTRA TERRESTRIAL INTELLIGENCE

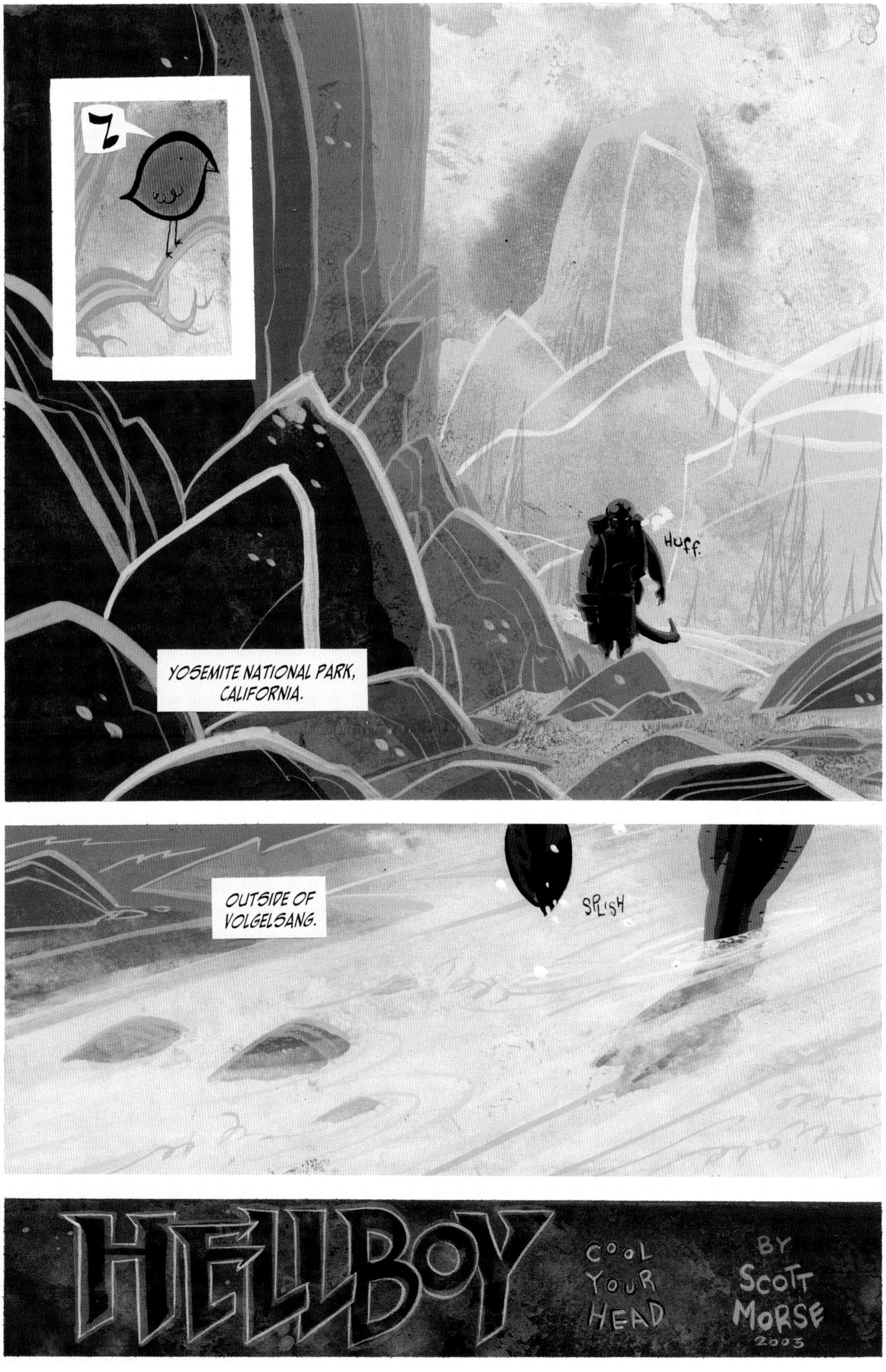
Z
YOSEMITE NATIONAL PARK, CALIFORNIA.
HUFF.
OUTSIDE OF VOLGELSANG.
SPLISH
HELLBOY
COOL YOUR HEAD
BY SCOTT MORSE 2003

101

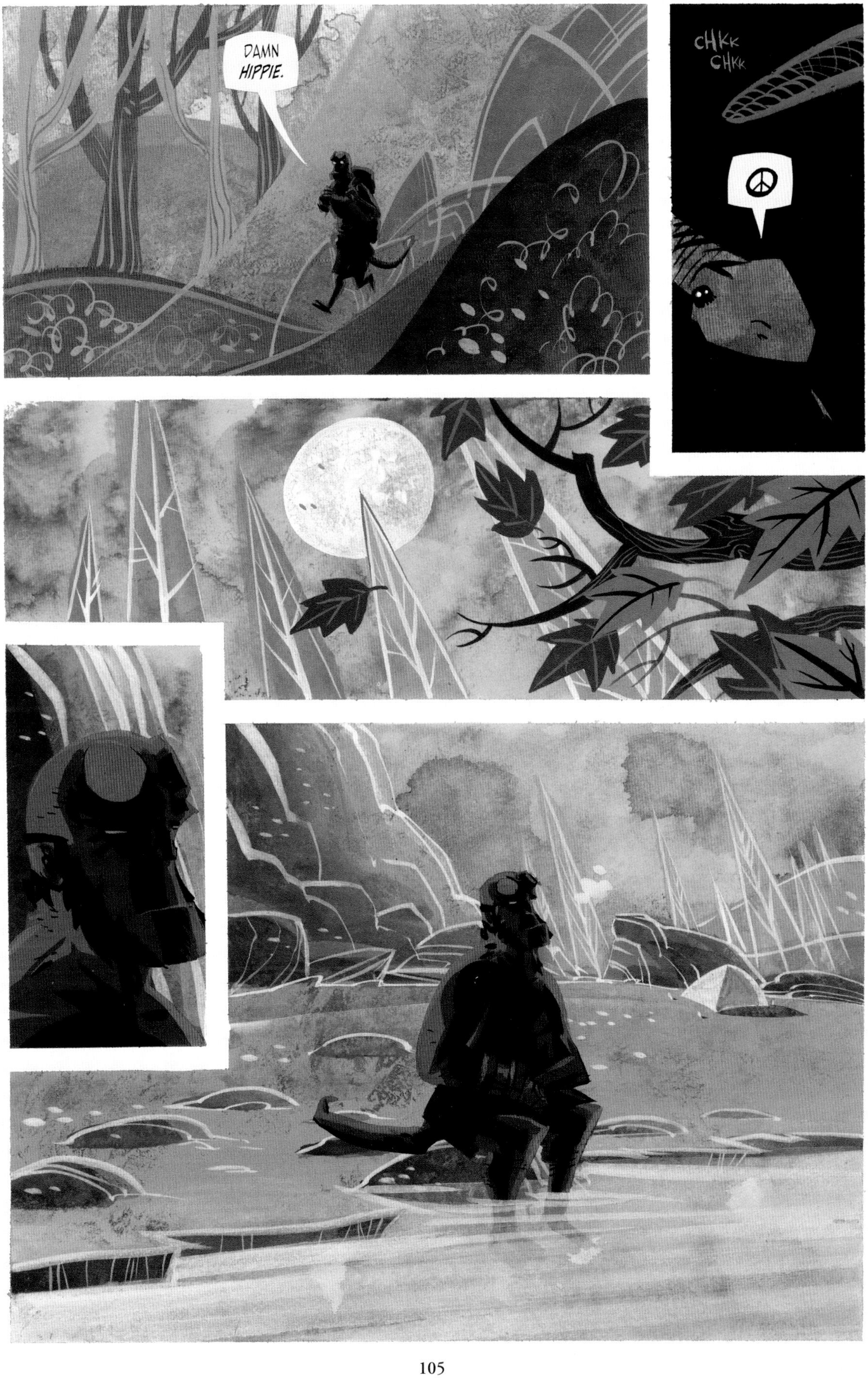
DAMN HIPPIE.
CHKK CHKK

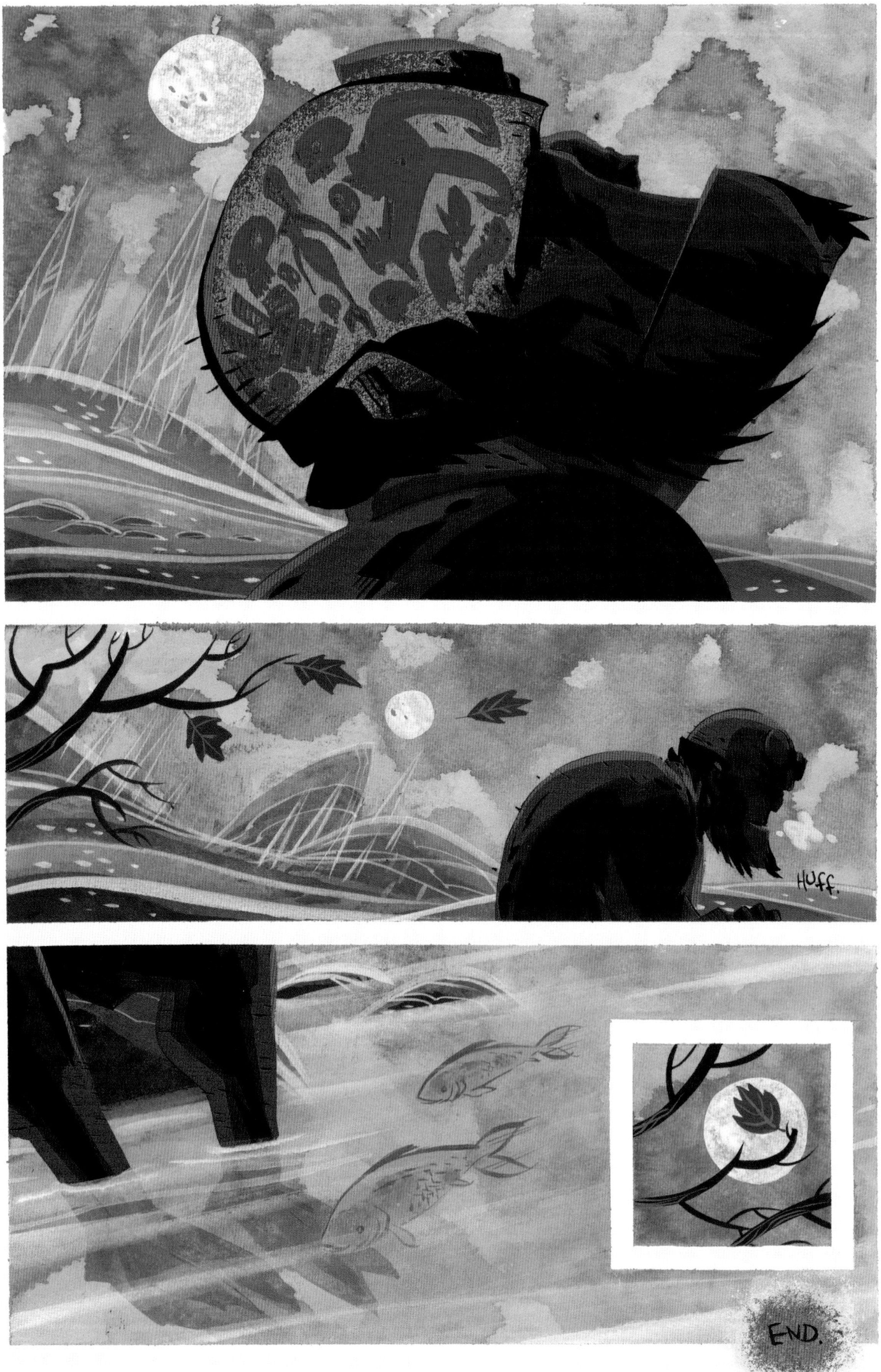
HUFF.
END.

Afterword

IN THE MID 1970s, I was in high school in Oakland, California. I don't remember much about that—not because of drugs or anything, I just have a lousy memory. What I *do* remember from that time was hunting through used bookstores with my brothers. Almost every weekend we took the bus (the 59 or the 76, then the College Avenue 51) into Berkeley and spent long hours looking for stuff. Those were good days. I don't remember exactly what my brothers were buying. Todd (the youngest) was reading a lot of Edgar Rice Burroughs in those days. Scott (the middle) went from Tolkien to "strange but true" stories of UFOs and the Bermuda Triangle. Little by little they spent less time in the bookstores and more time in the used record stores. For me it was always about the books. Ghost- and horror-story anthologies. And the two magic words I was looking for … *Weird Tales*.

I'm not sure when I first learned that there had been a pulp magazine called *Weird Tales*. There must have been some mention of it in Marvel Comics' *Savage Tales* or *Savage Sword of Conan*. Reading those magazines led me to reading the Conan books, then everything I could get my hands on by Robert E. Howard and his *Weird Tales* contemporaries. The '70s was a horrible time for fashion, but a great time for affordable pulp reprints, especially if you bought them used. For a while there it seemed I was discovering new (old, mostly dead, but new to me) authors every trip in those beautiful, dusty, cluttered, half-lit Berkeley book caves. I could go on and on about those places (Pendragon, Pellucidar, Moe's, Other Change of Hobbit, etc.), but the important thing here is that I was *reading* all that *Weird Tales* stuff. The almost science-fiction cosmic horror of Lovecraft. The weird fantasy of Clark Ashton Smith. The Seabury Quinn occult-detective stories. Henry Whitehead, Frank Bellknap Long, August Derleth, Price, Jacobi, Wellman, Brennan. Vampires, werewolves, lost worlds, mad scientists, giant amoebas, and rampaging fungi. I read a lot of great stuff, and I read a lot of crap. I absorbed it all—and twenty years later, it all came back out as *Hellboy*.

A couple of years ago, Scott Allie and I were racking our brains trying to come up with a title for this *Hellboy* anthology series. I kept saying that it had to be something like *Weird Tales*. Here we had a wide variety of creators producing a wide variety of supernatural stories (like *Weird Tales*), and, through Hellboy, they all owed something to that long-ago pulp-magazine icon. In the end we agreed that no sound-alike title was good enough. My thanks to Scott Allie for doing whatever he needed to secure the *Weird Tales* title, and to the powers that be at Dark Horse for letting him do it. I am thrilled and honored to see the words *Hellboy* and *Weird Tales* linked together, officially, at last.

MIKE MIGNOLA

Mike Mignola
New York City

HELLBOY™

G A L L E R Y

featuring

FRANK CHO
colored by DAVE STEWART

MICHAEL WM. KALUTA

PHIL NOTO

J.H. WILLIAMS III

CAMERON STEWART

GARY FIELDS
colored by MICHELLE MADSEN

BEN TEMPLESMITH

DAVE STEVENS
colored by DAVE STEWART
and

STEVE PURCELL

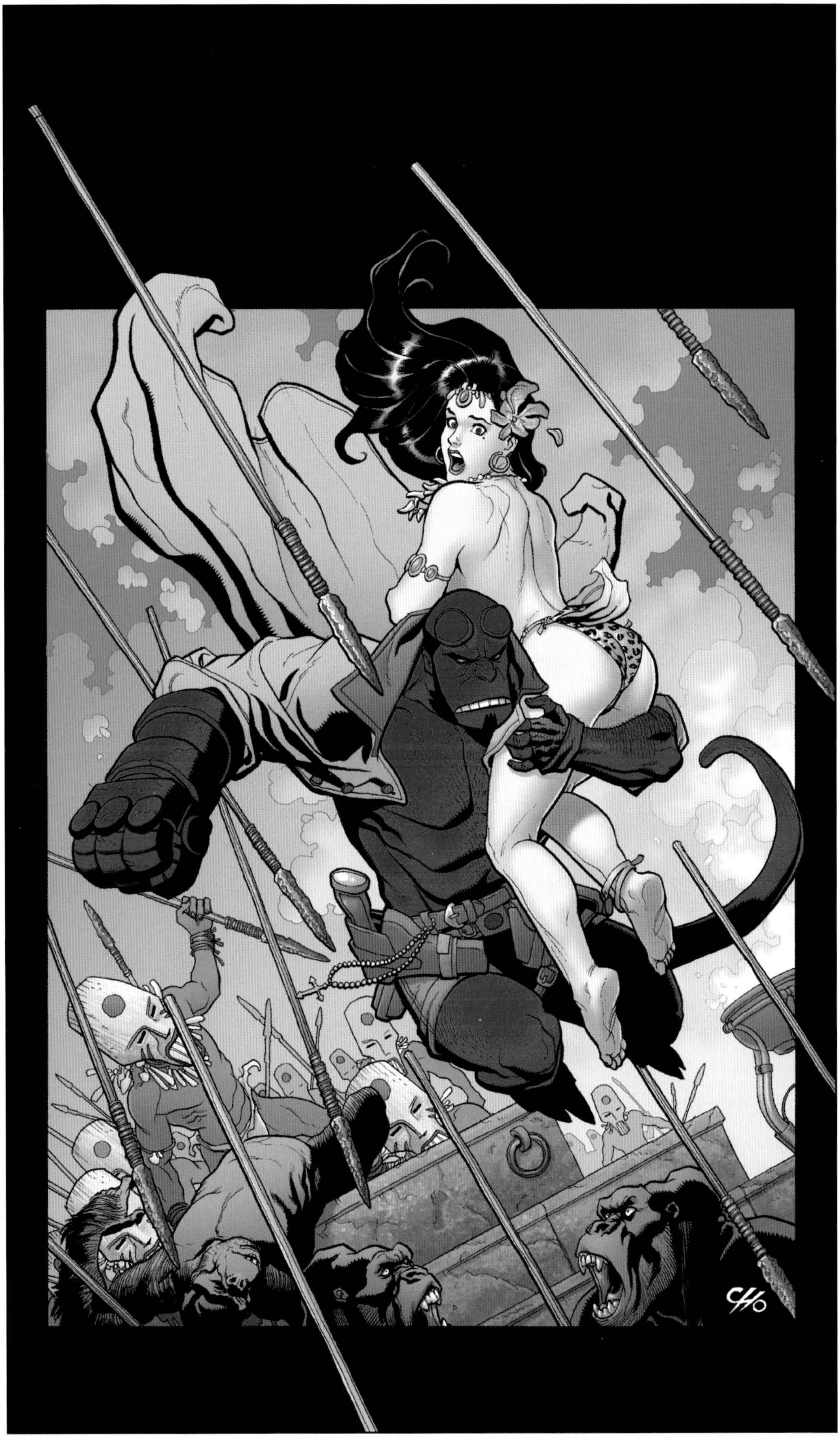

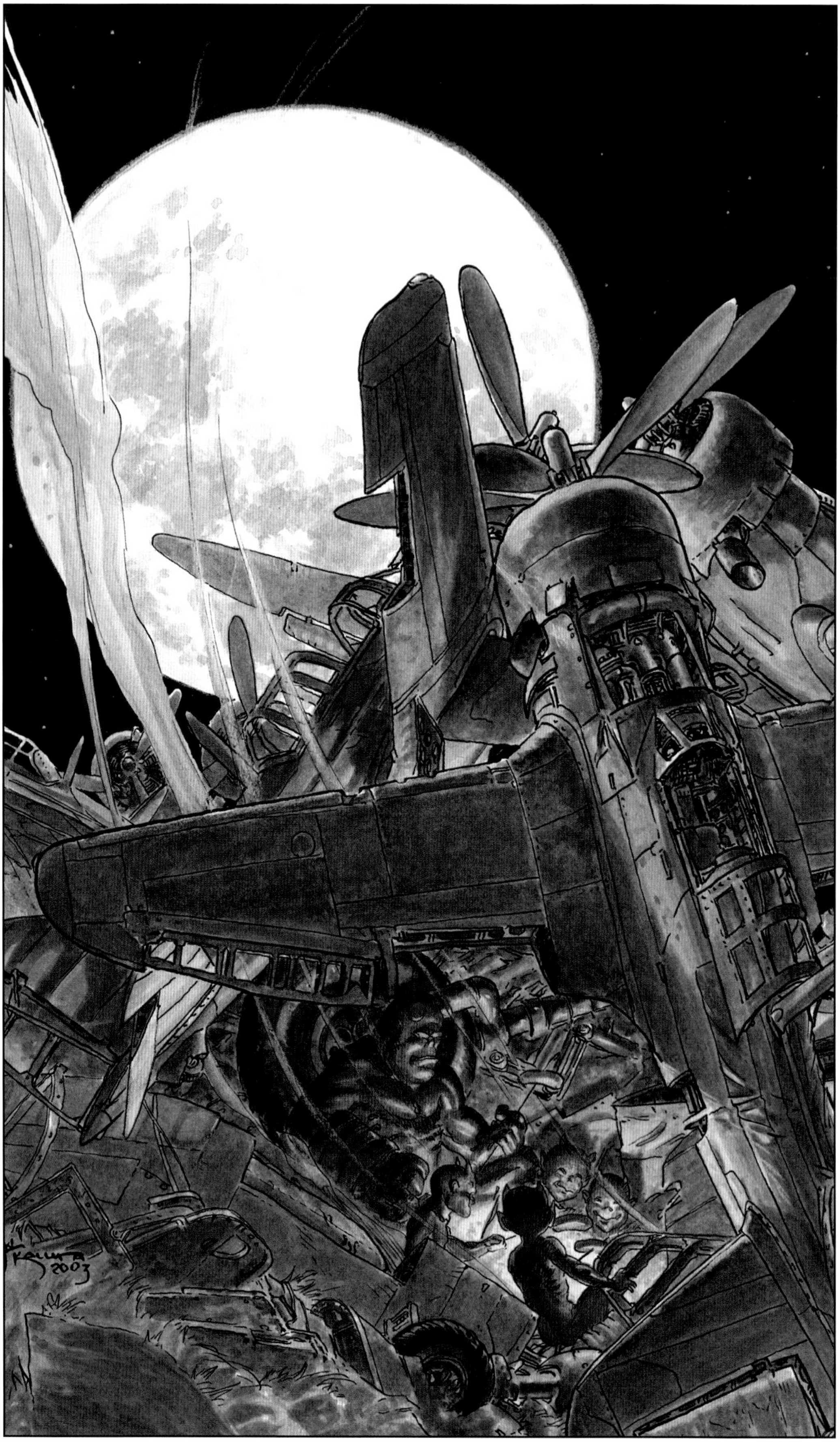
KALUTA
2003

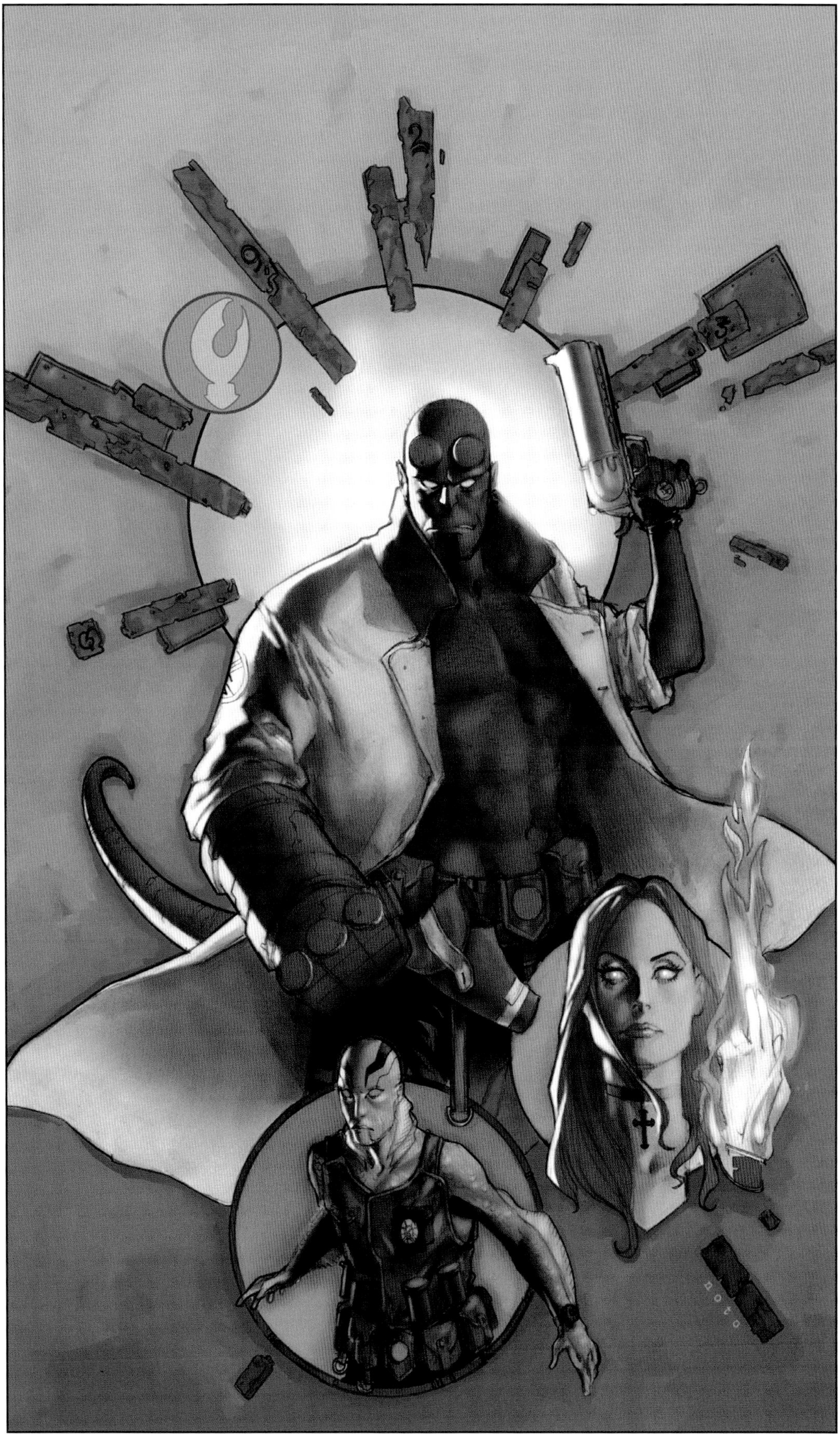

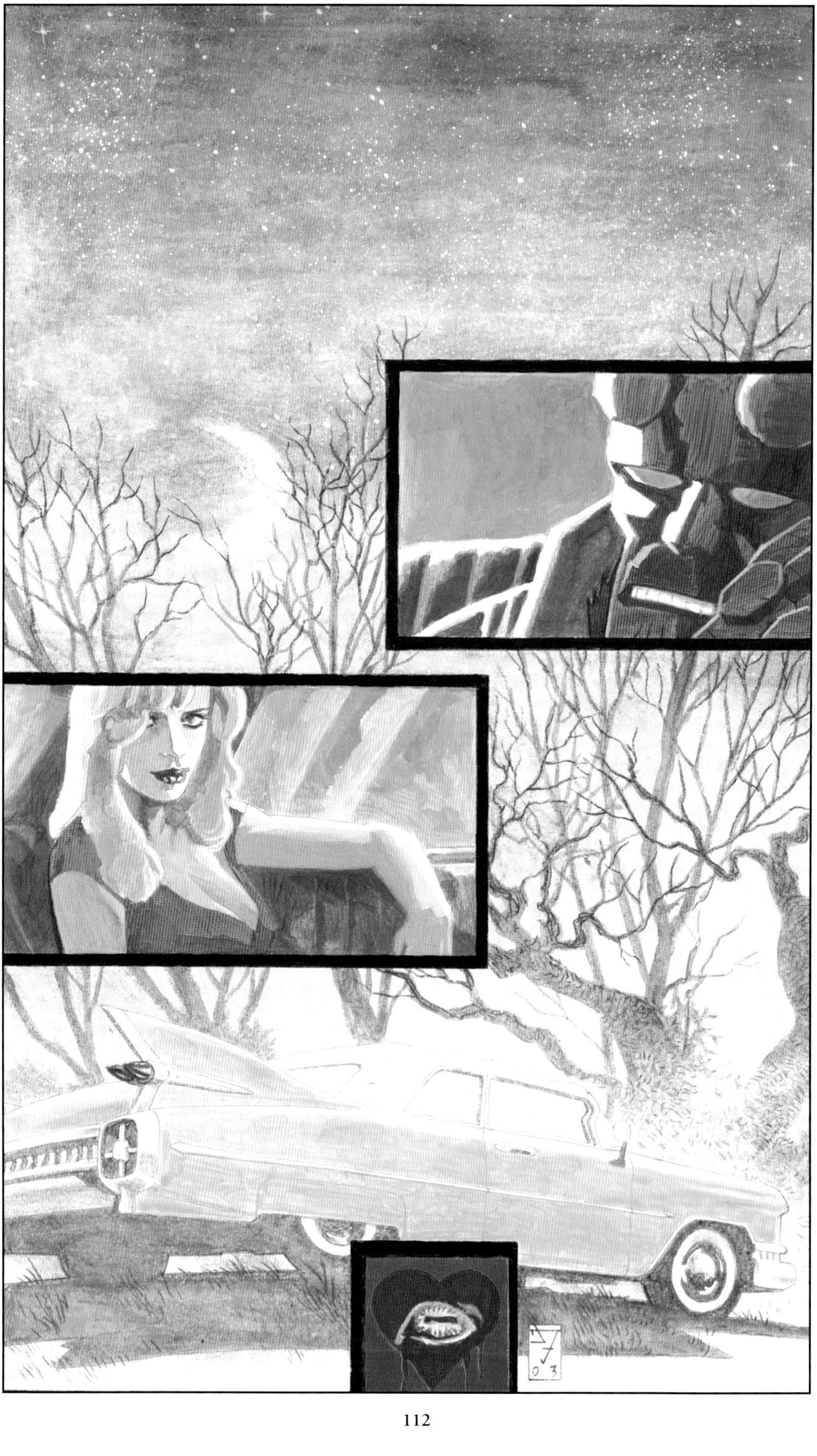

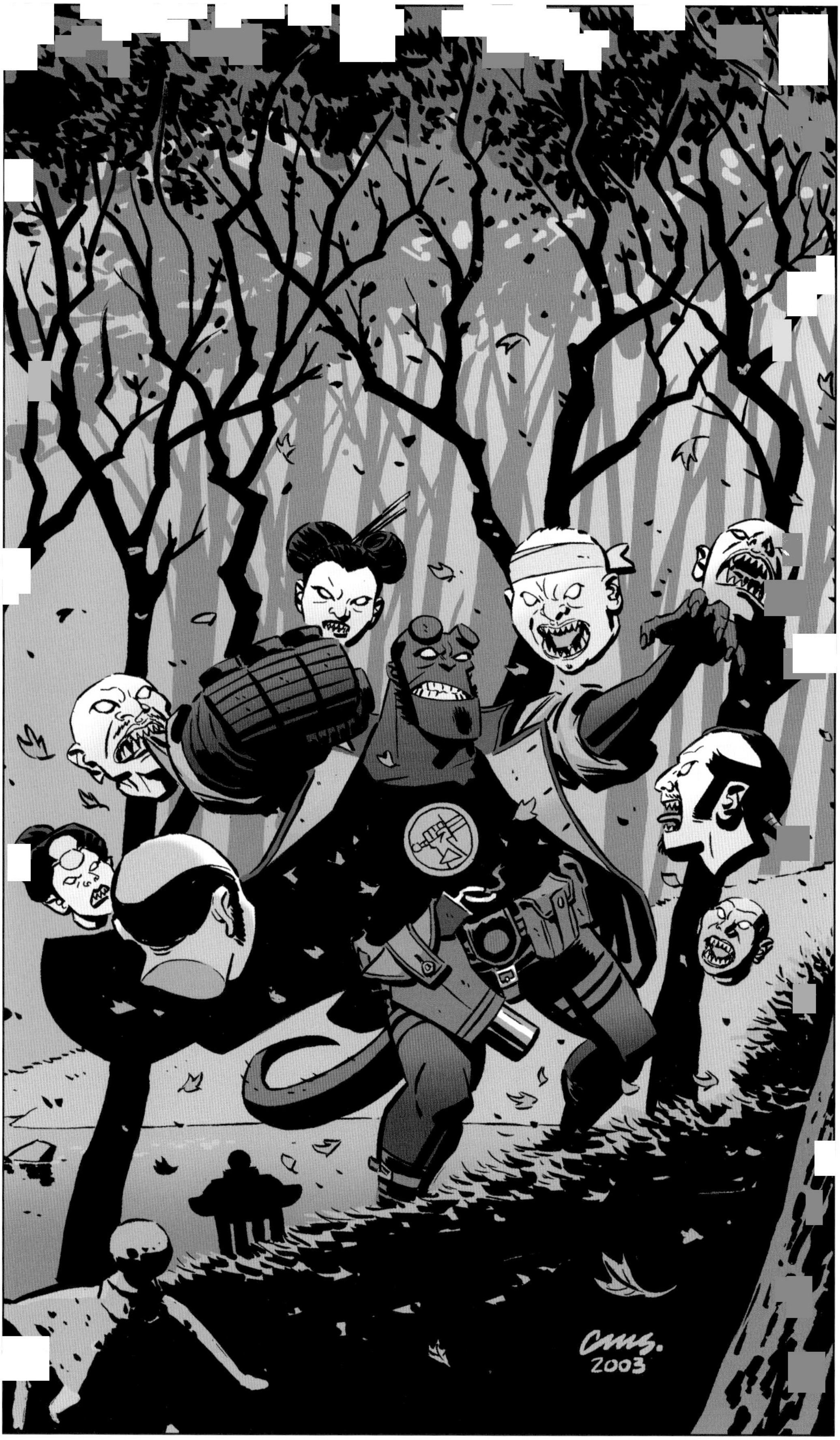
2003

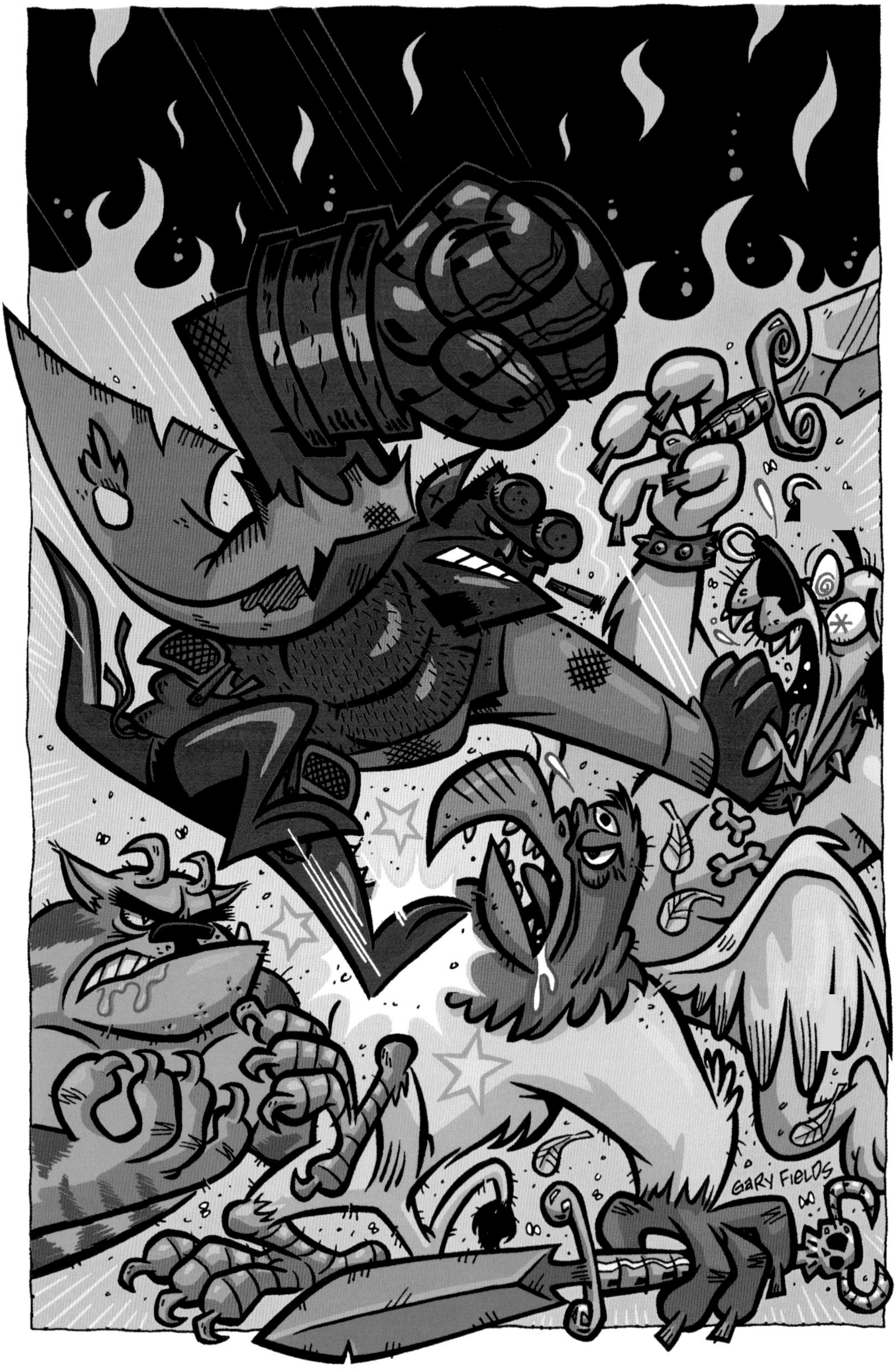
GARY FIELDS

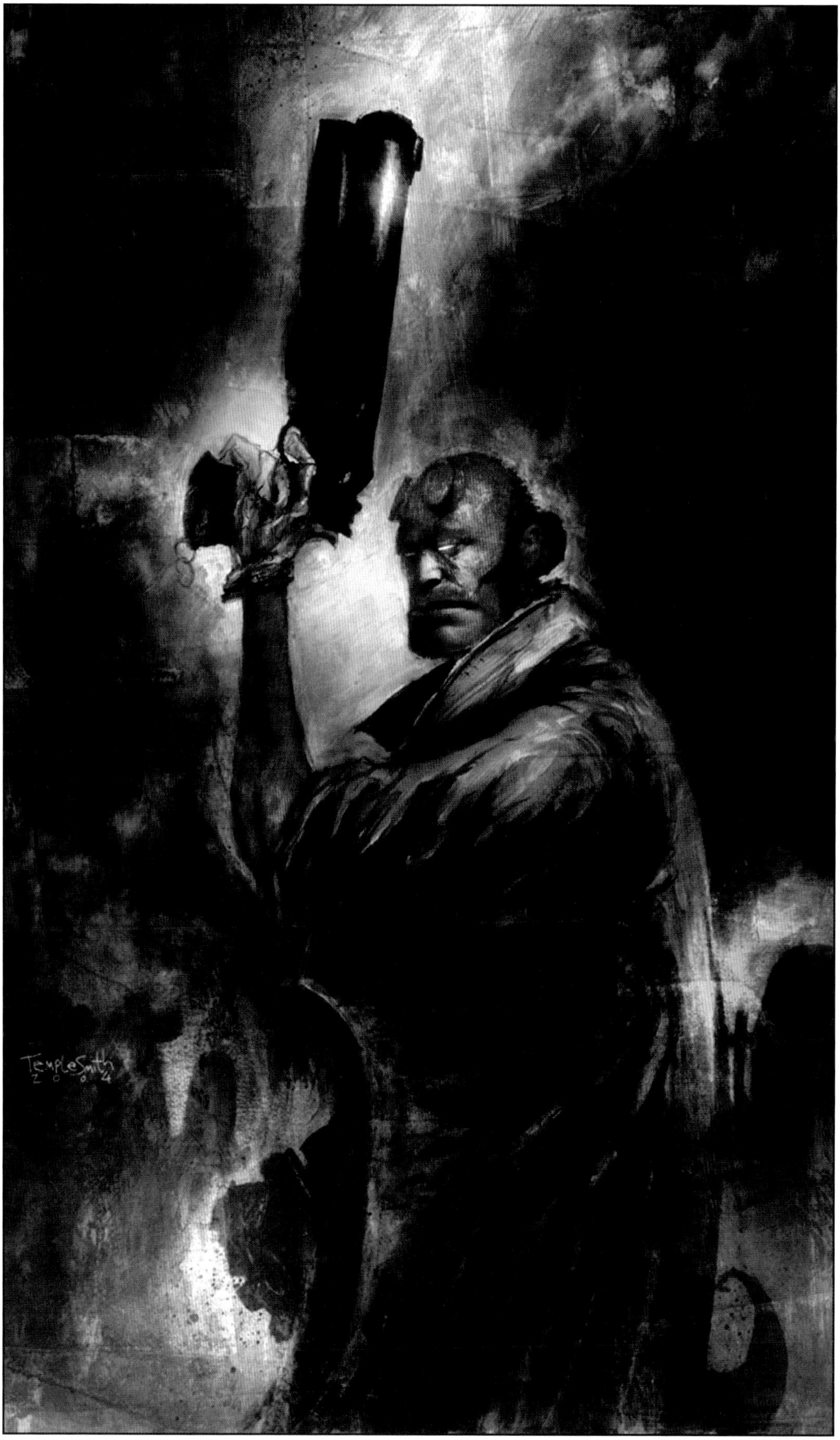
TempleSmith
2004

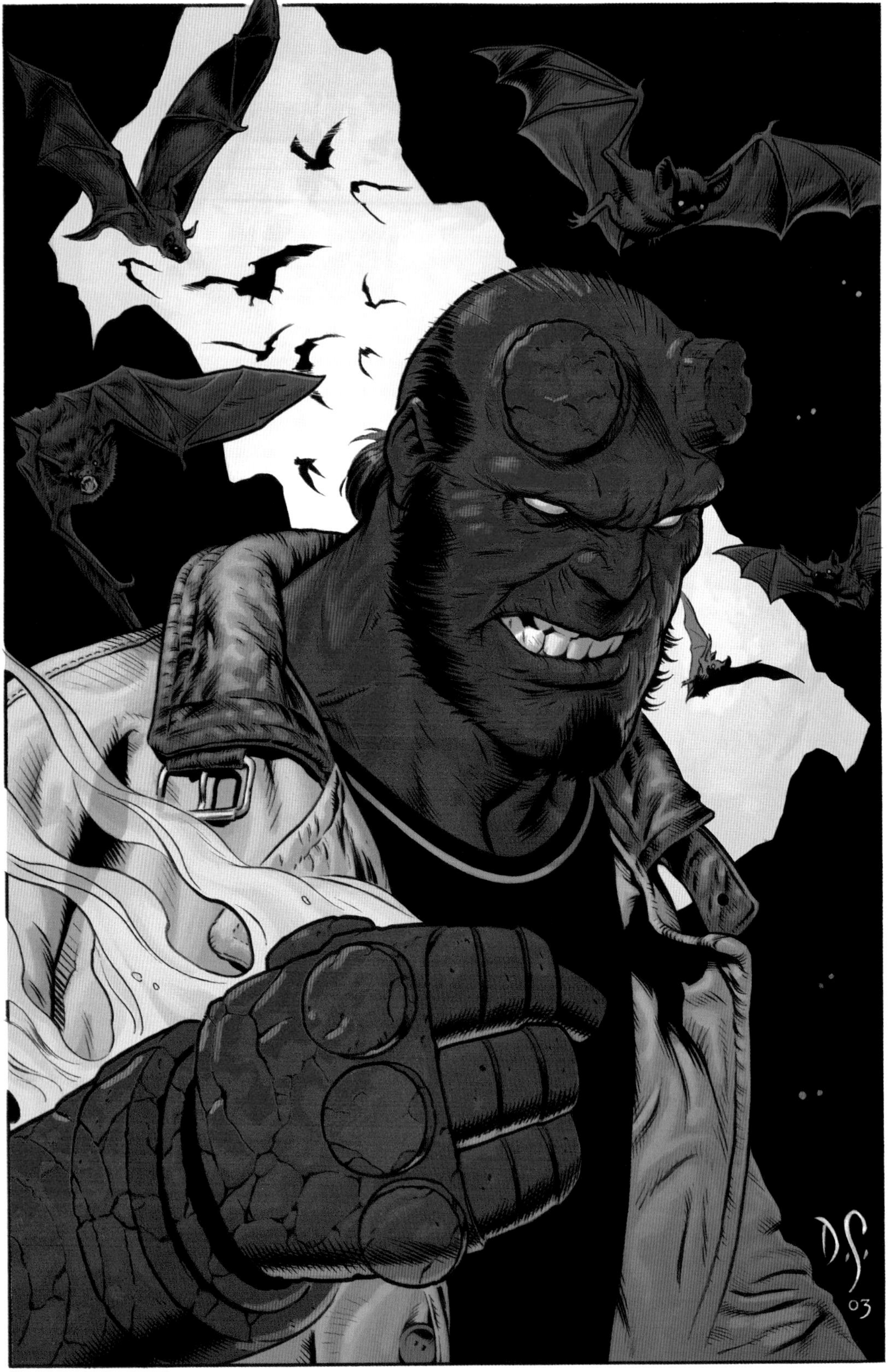

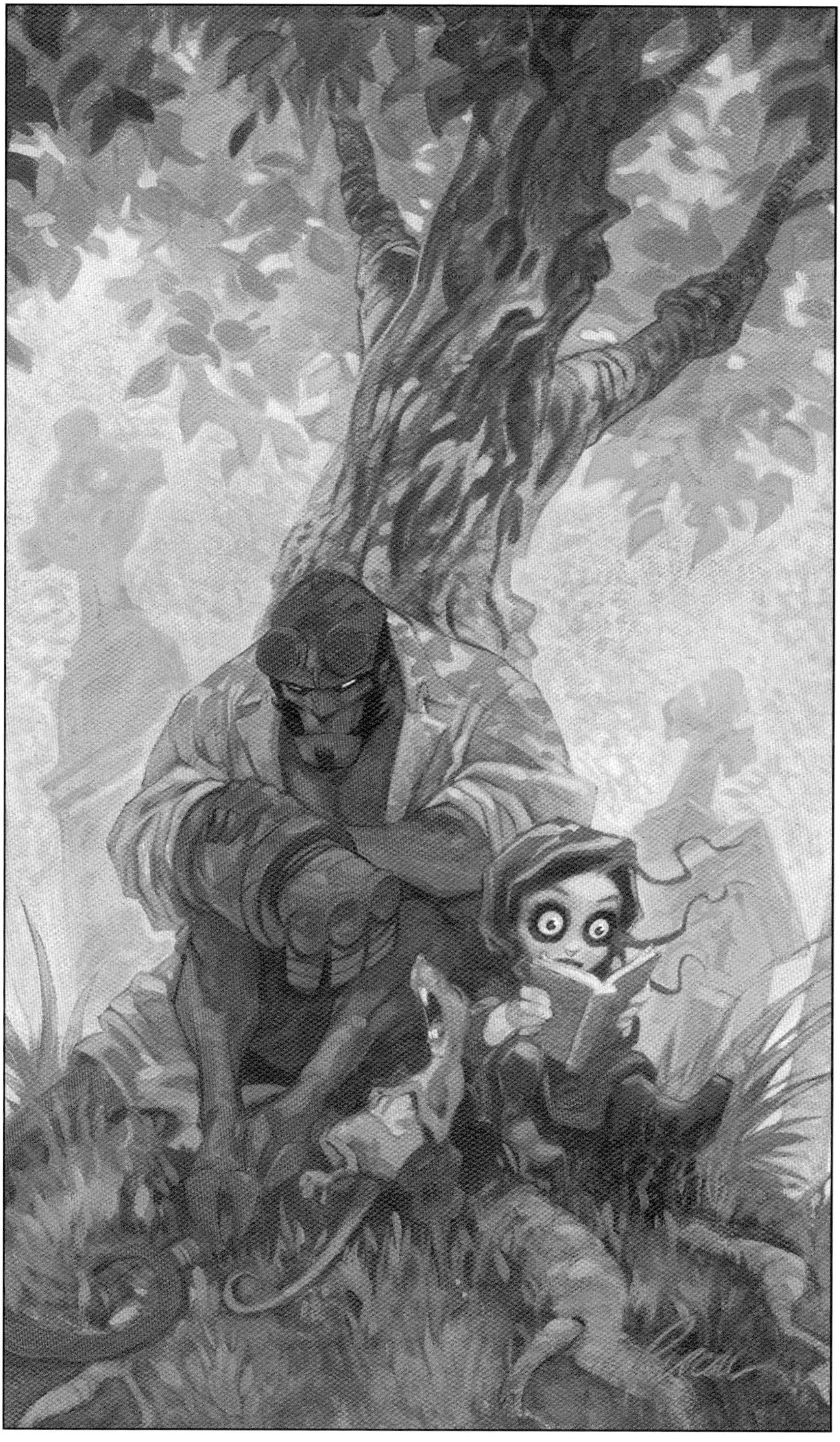

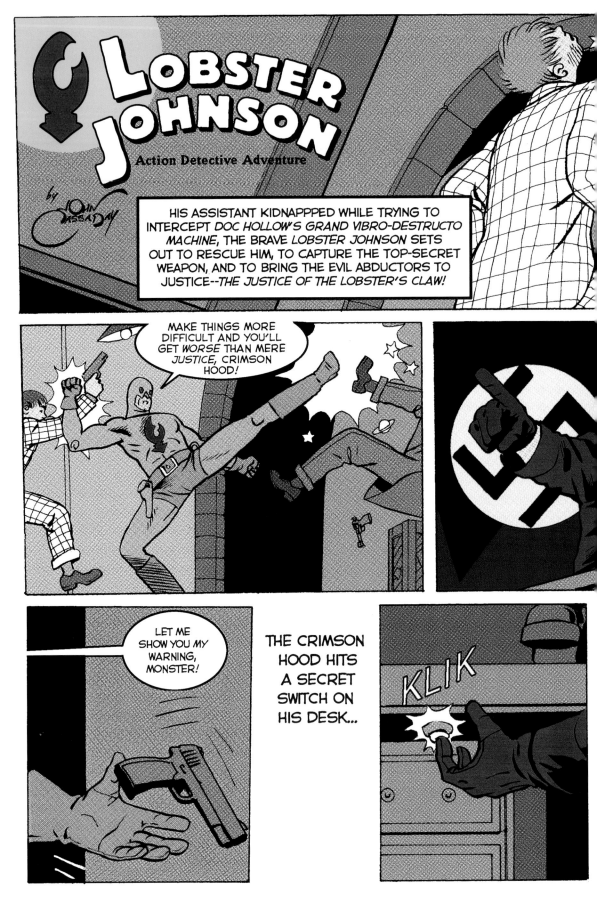

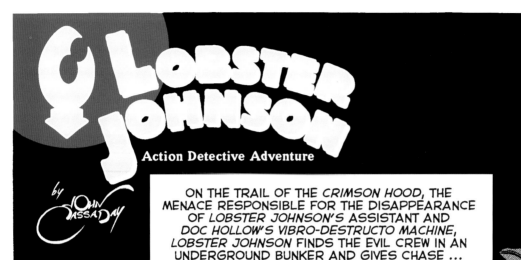

LOBSTER JOHNSON

Action Detective Adventure

by John Cassaday

ON THE TRAIL OF THE *CRIMSON HOOD*, THE MENACE RESPONSIBLE FOR THE DISAPPEARANCE OF *LOBSTER JOHNSON'S* ASSISTANT AND *DOC HOLLOW'S VIBRO-DESTRUCTO MACHINE*, *LOBSTER JOHNSON* FINDS THE EVIL CREW IN AN UNDERGROUND BUNKER AND GIVES CHASE ...

UNABLE TO PREVENT THE HOODED VILLAIN'S ESCAPE, THE *CRUSTACEOUS AVENGER* INTERROGATES ONE OF THE HENCHMEN, LEFT BEHIND TO FACE THE *JUSTICE* OF THE *LOBSTER'S CLAW!*

GO CLIMB UP YER THUMB! I KNOW FROM NOTHIN'!

YOU DAISY RAT!

BANG

SCUM!

BLAM

120

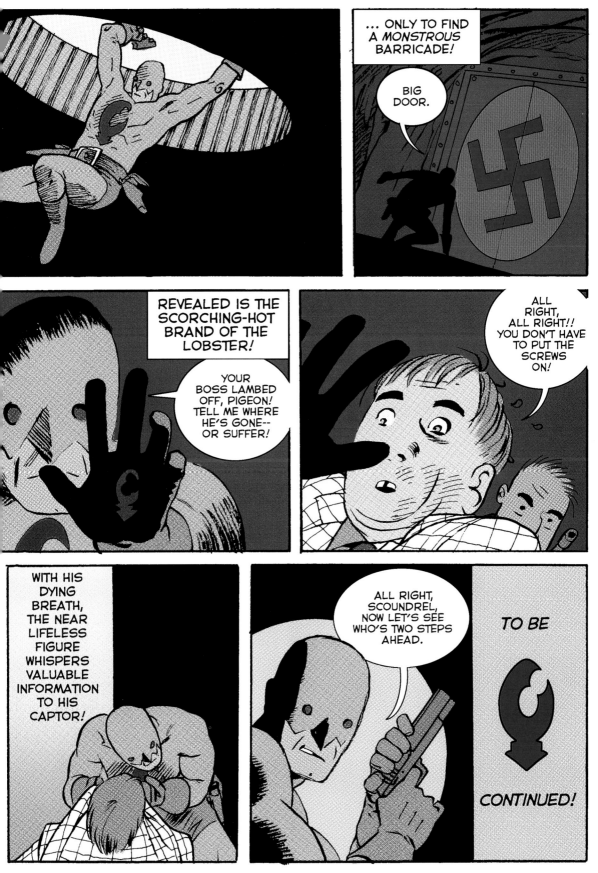

122

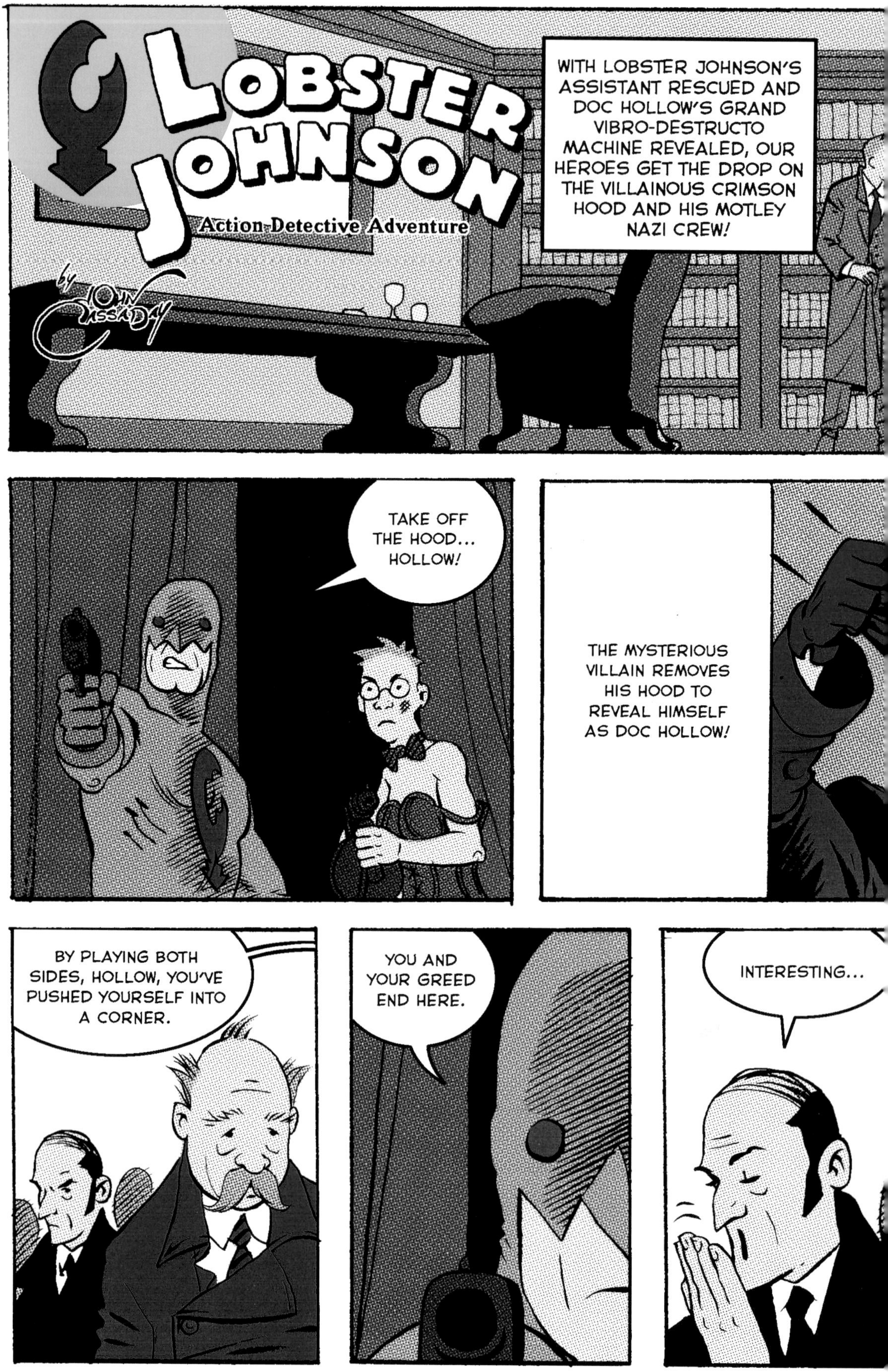
LOBSTER JOHNSON
Action-Detective Adventure
WITH LOBSTER JOHNSON'S ASSISTANT RESCUED AND DOC HOLLOW'S GRAND VIBRO-DESTRUCTO MACHINE REVEALED, OUR HEROES GET THE DROP ON THE VILLAINOUS CRIMSON HOOD AND HIS MOTLEY NAZI CREW!
TAKE OFF THE HOOD... HOLLOW!
THE MYSTERIOUS VILLAIN REMOVES HIS HOOD TO REVEAL HIMSELF AS DOC HOLLOW!
BY PLAYING BOTH SIDES, HOLLOW, YOU'VE PUSHED YOURSELF INTO A CORNER.
YOU AND YOUR GREED END HERE.
INTERESTING...

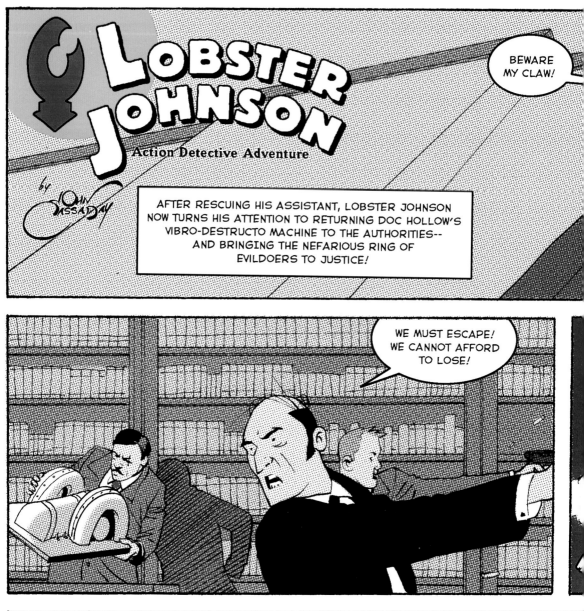

LOBSTER JOHNSON

Action Detective Adventure

by John Cassaday

BEWARE MY CLAW!

AFTER RESCUING HIS ASSISTANT, LOBSTER JOHNSON NOW TURNS HIS ATTENTION TO RETURNING DOC HOLLOW'S VIBRO-DESTRUCTO MACHINE TO THE AUTHORITIES-- AND BRINGING THE NEFARIOUS RING OF EVILDOERS TO JUSTICE!

WE MUST ESCAPE! WE CANNOT AFFORD TO LOSE!

CRUNCH!

THE MACHINE, SMASHED, SUDDENLY COMES TO LIFE AND BEGINS TO VIBRATE...

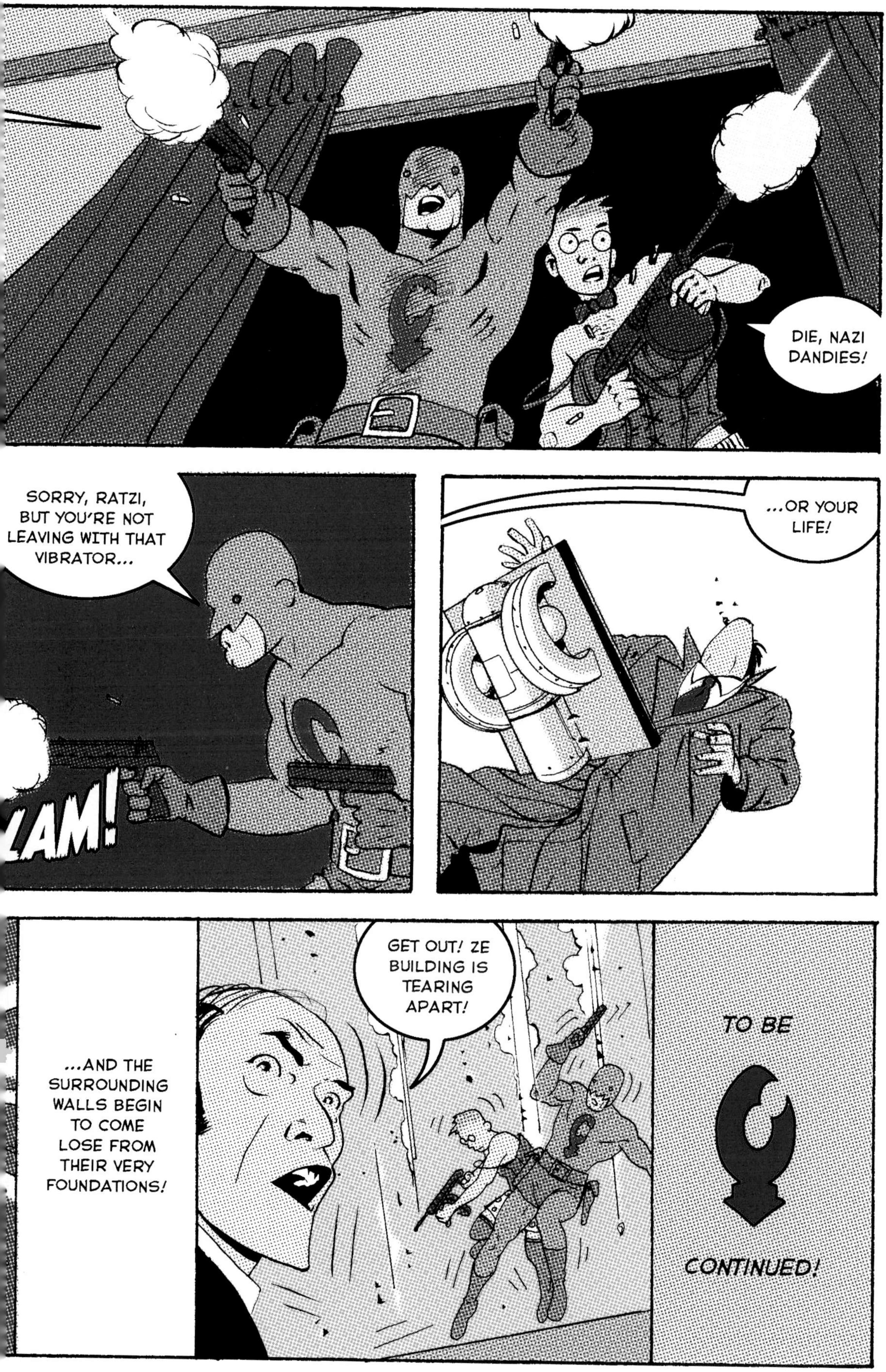
DIE, NAZI DANDIES!
SORRY, RATZI, BUT YOU'RE NOT LEAVING WITH THAT VIBRATOR...
LAM!
...OR YOUR LIFE!
...AND THE SURROUNDING WALLS BEGIN TO COME LOSE FROM THEIR VERY FOUNDATIONS!
GET OUT! ZE BUILDING IS TEARING APART!
TO BE
CONTINUED!

THE VIBRATIONS OF THE TOP-SECRET WEAPON BRING THE THE MANSION WALLS CRUMBLING TO THE GROUND! WILL OUR HERO AND HIS ASSISTANT ESCAPE IN TIME??

133

SKETCHBOOK

The following pages feature a special in-depth look at the roughs and studies of two very different *Weird Tales* artists.

P. Craig Russell

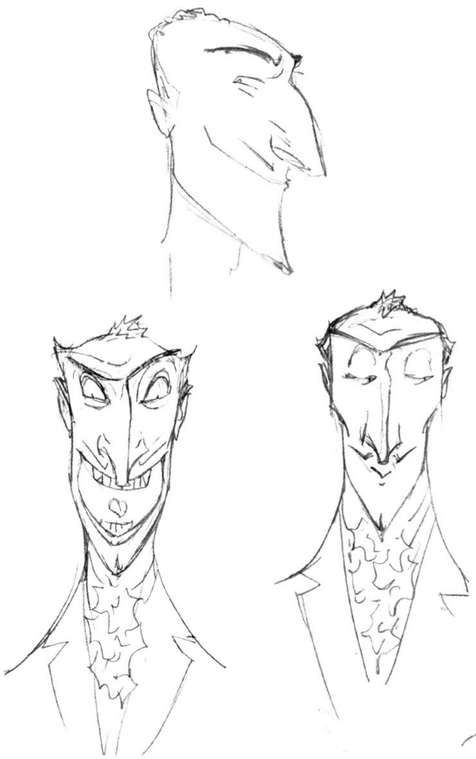

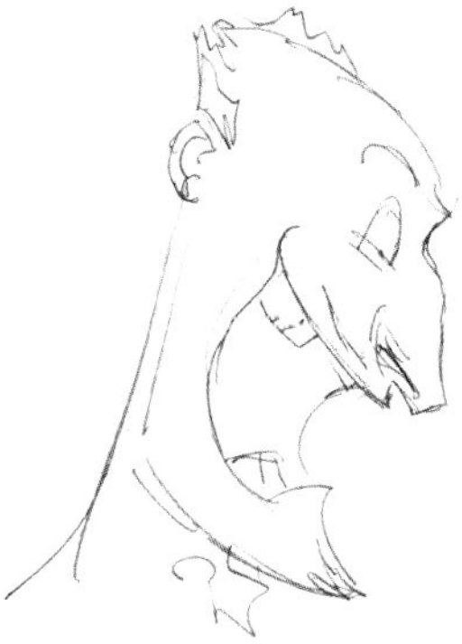

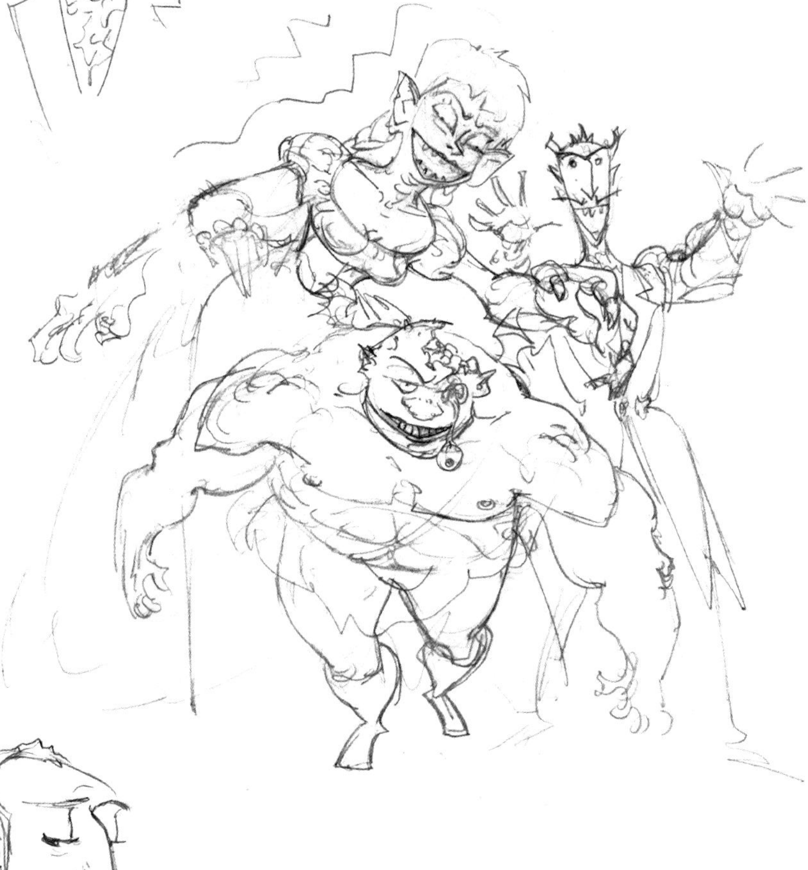

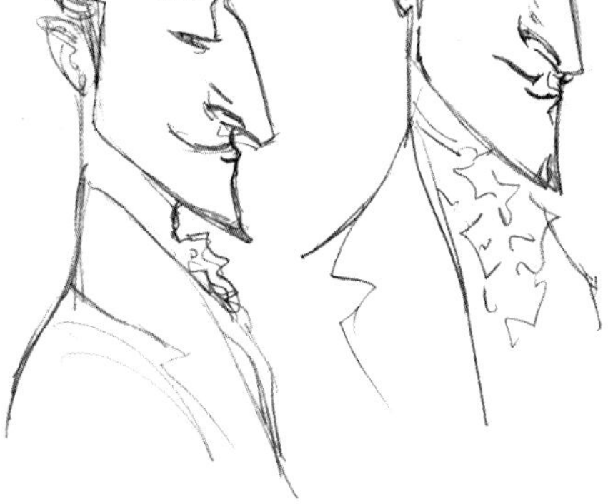

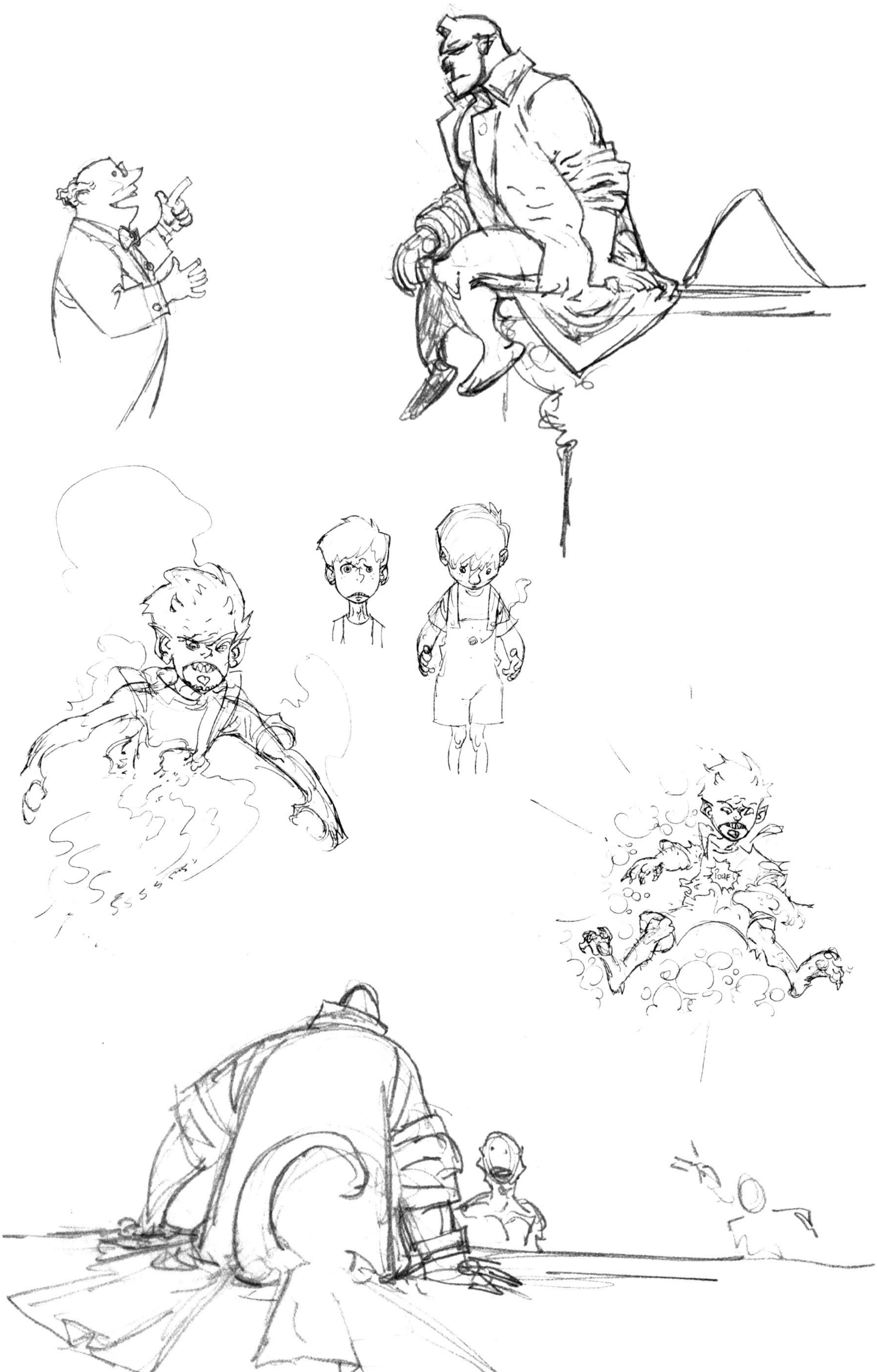
POUF

Evan Dorkin

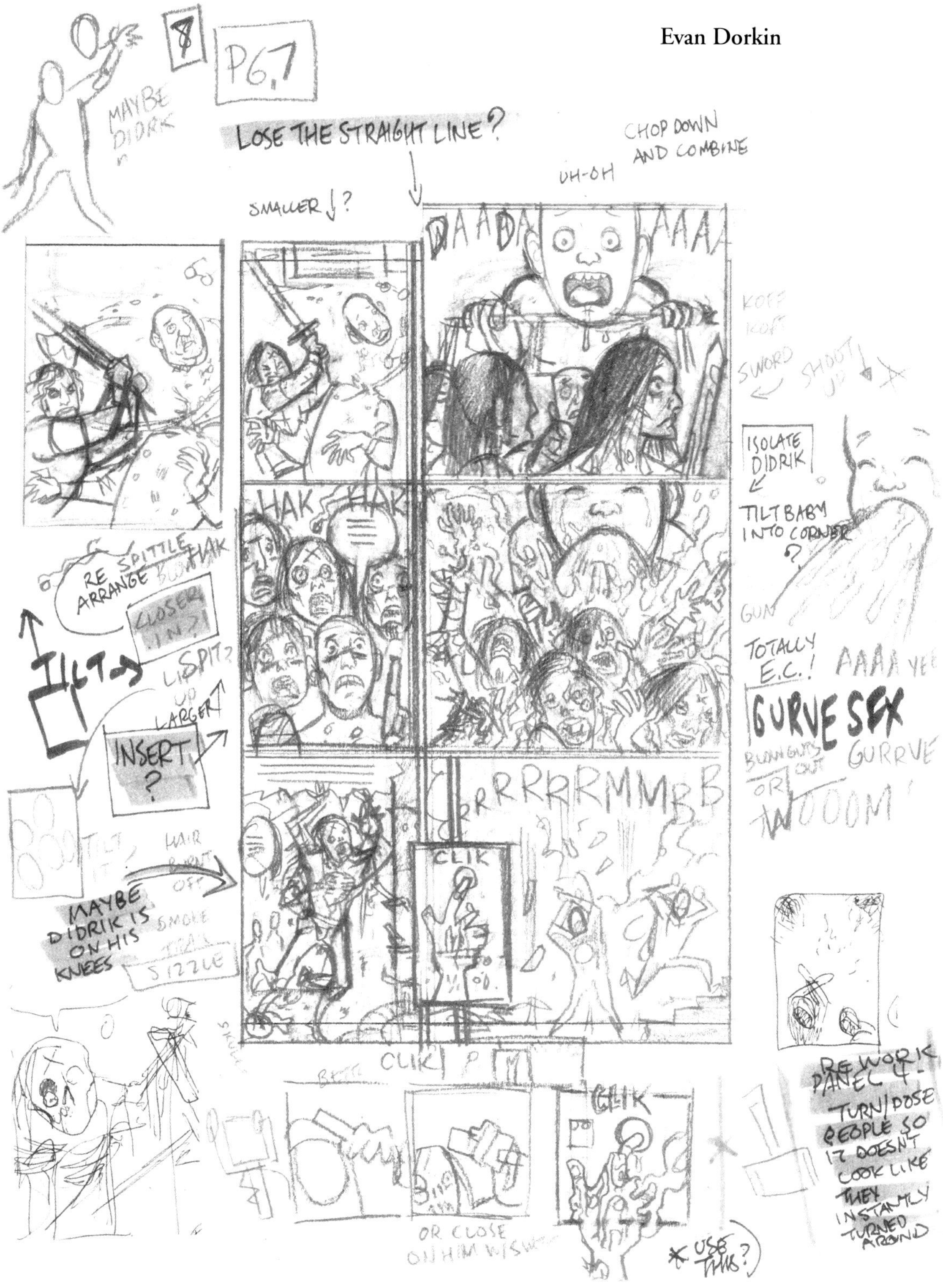
P6,7
MAYBE DIDRK
LOSE THE STRAIGHT LINE?
CHOP DOWN AND COMBINE
UH-OH
SMALLER ↓?
DAAA AAAA
KOFF KOFF
SWORD
SHOOT UP
ISOLATE DIDRIK
TILT BABY INTO CORNER ?
HAK HAK
RE ARRANGE SPITTLE
CLOSER IN?
TILT
SPIT? UP LARGER
INSERT ?
GUN
TOTALLY E.C.!
AAAA YEE
GURVE SEX
GURRVE
OR WOOOM
RRRRRRMMBB
CLIK
HAIR BURNT OFF
MAYBE DIDRIK IS ON HIS KNEES
SMOKE TRAIL
SIZZLE
CLIK
CLIK
OR CLOSE ON HIM W/SW
* USE THIS?
REWORK PANEL 4 - TURN/POSE PEOPLE SO IT DOESN'T LOOK LIKE THEY INSTANTLY TURNED AROUND

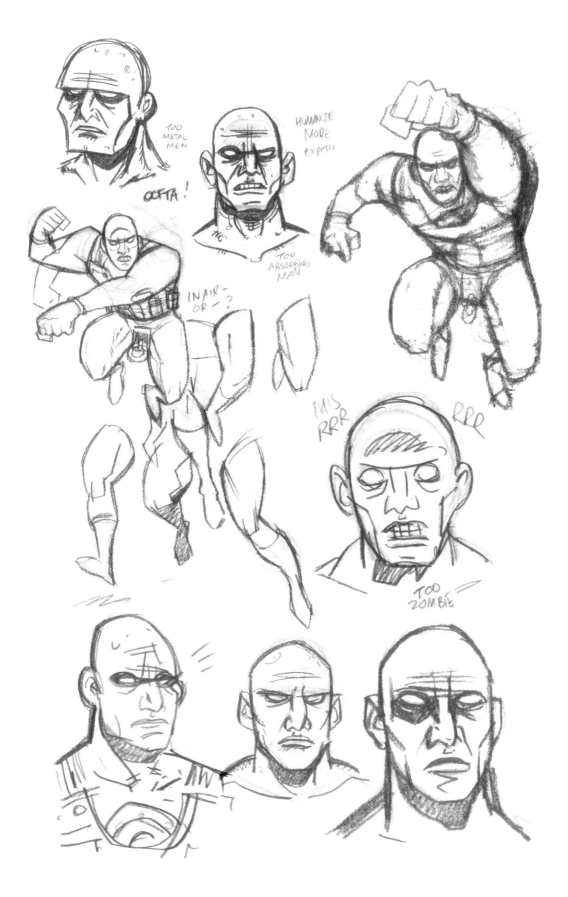

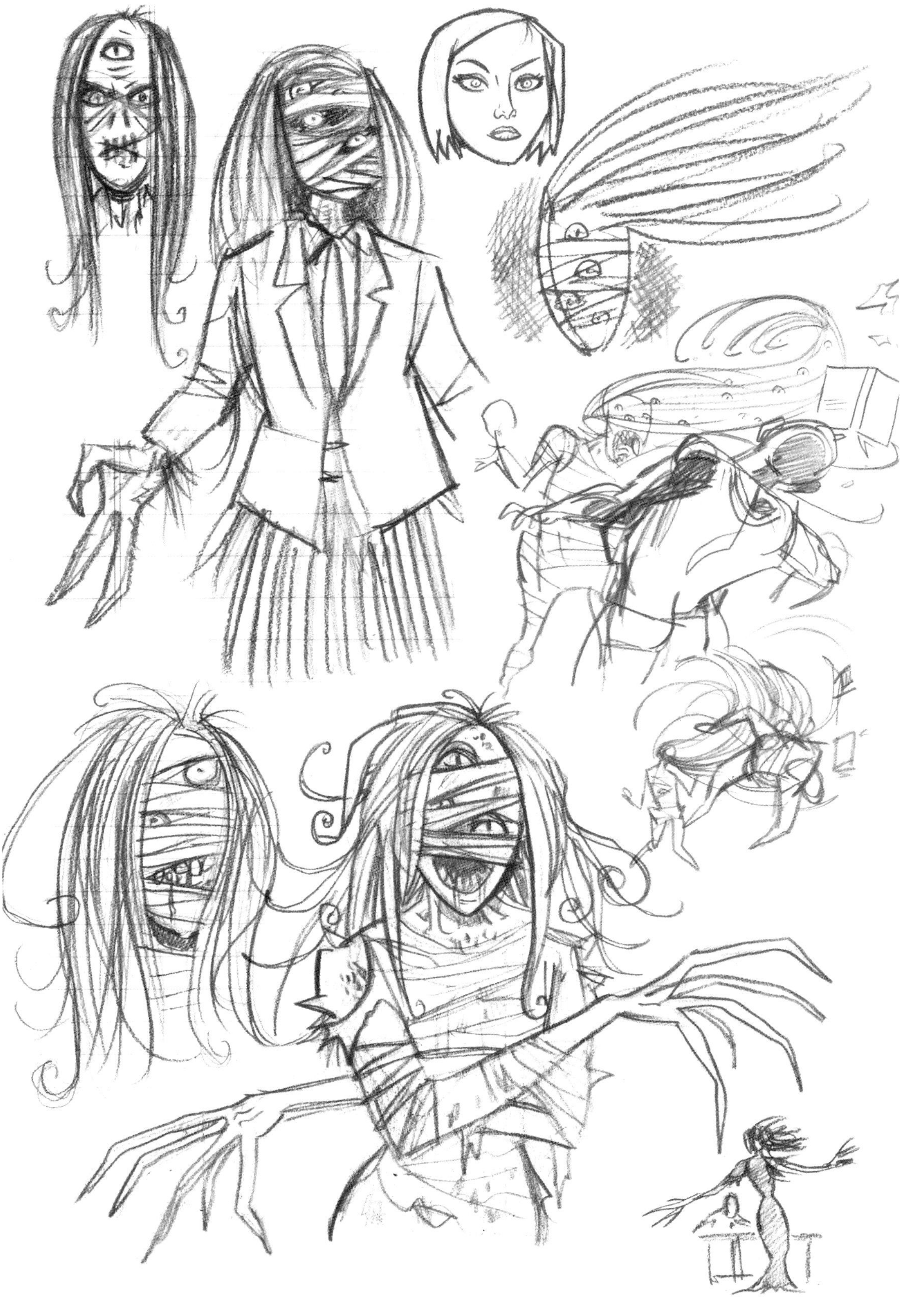

CREATORS

KIA ASAMIYA is one of Japan's foremost manga illustrators. Born in Tokyo in 1963, Mr. Asamiya has written and illustrated literally dozens of novel-length mangas, which are as popular with readers today as they were when they were originally issued. His work includes such classics as *Silent Moebius, Steam Detectives, Martian Successor Nadesico, Compiler, Dark Angel,* and many others. Many of his works have been adapted for animated television series and motion pictures, and his manga are regularly reprinted by publishers the world over.

LEE BERMEJO was born in Athens, Ohio, but spent the majority of his life living in southern California. After an extended internship at Wildstorm Studios he began working on small miniseries and fill-ins for both Wildstorm and DC, such as *Superman/Gen13, Batman/Deathblow, Hellblazer, and Global Frequency.* Now twenty-six, Lee lives in San Diego and is hard at work on *Lex Luthor: Man of Steel* for DC Comics. He considers the opportunity to work on a Hellboy image to be one of the high points of his short career thus far.

W. HADEN BLACKMAN has been hunting monsters since he was five. He is the author of *The Field Guide to North American Monsters* and *The Field Guide to North American Hauntings,* along with numerous comic-book stories for Dark Horse. He is primarily nocturnal and has yet to be photographed in the wild.

JOHN CASSADAY never got to live his dream of replacing Slayer guitarist Kerry King. Still, he did become a highly respected professional comic-book artist, and that's not so bad for a long-haired kid from Texas. His works to date include acclaimed stints on *Desperadoes, Captain America,* and *Planetary.*

FRANK CHO is a self-taught artist-writer and the creator of the highly successful comic strip *Liberty Meadows.* Cho has won many awards including: the prestigious National Cartoonist Society's Awards for Best Comic Book and Book Illustration, the Charles M. Schulz Award for Excellence in Cartooning, Scripps-Howard Award for Best College Cartoonist, College Media Association for Cartooning, and Germany's highest award, the Max & Moritz Medal, for Best International Comic Strip. He has been nominated for the coveted Harvey and Eisner Awards numerous times. Frank Cho currently lives in Elkridge, Maryland with his wife Cari, daughters Emily and Samantha, and their wiener dog Truman.

Bronx native GENE COLAN has been a permanent fixture in the comics industry since 1946, and now his cinematic work is often published directly from pencils. Long associated with such popular characters as Dracula, Daredevil, Batman, Howard the Duck, Captain America, Wonder Woman, Sub-Mariner, Dr. Strange, Silver Surfer, and many others, Colan is comfortable illustrating numerous genres and has taught at both the School of Visual Arts in Manhattan and the Fashion Institute of Technology. Colan currently lives in Florida with his wife Adrienne.

EVAN DORKIN is the Harvey, Eisner, and Ignatz Award-winning creator of *Milk and Cheese* and *Dork* from Slave Labor Graphics, and various Marvel, Dark Horse, and DC comics. His cartooning has appeared in *Esquire, Spin, The Onion, MAD,* and *Nickelodeon* magazine. With Sarah Dyer, he's written for *Space Ghost Coast to Coast, Superman,* and *Batman Beyond,* and created *Welcome to Eltingville,* his very own failed pilot that aired on Cartoon Network's Adult Swim block. He is currently working on his next failed pilot for them.

TOMMY LEE EDWARDS has created art and told stories all his life. He has created promotion and product art for the *Harry Potter, Men in Black* and *Dinotopia* films, *Star Wars* children's books, conceptual and storyboard work for *Sinbad: Legend of the Seven Seas*, game packaging for Hasbro, and comics such as *ZombieWorld, Batman*, and the upcoming *Question* series from Wildstorm-DC. Currently on Tommy's desk are a series of illustrations for the upcoming film *Batman Begins*, style-guide art for *Star Wars Episode III*, and storyboards and concept art for a sci-fi military game at Electronic Arts.

TOM FASSBENDER is the author of two pulp-fiction novels, a *Buffy the Vampire Slayer* illustrated novel, and a run of *Buffy* comics—all written with Jim Pascoe. Fassbender & Pascoe also own and run UglyTown, the country's premier crime-fiction book publisher.

After graduating from the Kubert School twenty years ago, **GARY FIELDS** has worked for almost every major comic-book publisher, done comic strips, children's books, *Cracked Magazine*, illustration, character design, gag cartoons, and animation work. He is currently working as a staff illustrator for the Children's Place. He also works for DC Comics on their Cartoon Network books, creates gags and comics for *Nickelodeon Magazine*, and anything else he can get his hands on.

MICHAEL WM. KALUTA took his first professional art assignment in 1969 for Charlton Comics. Within four years, his stunning fantasy/adventure work earned Kaluta what would soon become his signature job—a long run on the DC Comics series *The Shadow*. In the years since, Kaluta has spanned many worlds in both illustration and comics work—from the erotic comedy of *Starstruck*, which ran as a popular feature in *Heavy Metal*, to the art-book adaptation of Thea von Harbou's *Metropolis*.

RON MARZ was dragged into the comics industry fifteen years ago by his pal Jim Starlin. Since then, he's written numerous titles, including *Green Lantern* for DC, *Silver Surfer* for Marvel, and *Star Wars* for Dark Horse. But getting the chance to collaborate with Starlin on a Hellboy story is definitely one of the highlights.

SCOTT MORSE is the author of many graphic novels and short stories, including *Soulwind* (Oni Press), *The Barefoot Serpent* (Top Shelf Productions), *Southpaw* (AdHouse Books), and *Ancient Joe* (Dark Horse). In animation, he's acted as designer, storyboard artist, writer, art director, and producer for Univeral, Cartoon Network, Disney, and Nickelodeon. He lives in Burbank, California, but would rather be backpacking in Yosemite. He knows how to get to Hanging Basket, but it's a secret worth keeping, so don't ask for directions.

PHIL NOTO's comic work includes covers for DC's *Birds of Prey*, artist on Black Bull's *Beautiful Killer*, two *Danger Girl* specials for Wildstorm, and a story for Dark Horse's *Grendel: Black, White, and Red*. Phil previously worked as an assistant animator for Walt Disney Feature Animation for ten years where his credits included *Lion King, Mulan*, and *Lilo and Stitch*. He currently lives in Orlando, Florida with his wife, Beth.

JIM PASCOE is the author of two pulp-fiction novels, a *Buffy the Vampire Slayer* illustrated novel, and a slew of *Buffy* comics—all written with Tom Fassbender. Fassbender & Pascoe also own and run UglyTown, the country's premier crime-fiction book publisher. On the solo tip, Jim Pascoe's written

DOUG PETRIE loves Gene Colan and doesn't care who knows it. Petrie has written and directed episodes of *Buffy the Vampire Slayer* and written screenp[redacted] for *The Fantastic Four* and *Harriet the Spy*. [redacted] lives in Los Angeles with his wife Alexa and son Henry.

After honing his skills with the small-press satire *Violent Man*, WILL PFEIFER got his big break with the Vertigo mini-series *Finals*. Other credits include *Bizarro Comics, H-E-R-O, X-Men Unlimited, Space Ghost,* and *Batman: Black and White*. He lives in Illinois with his lovely and understanding wife, Amy. And, by day, he works for a great metropolitan newspaper (really!).

STEVE PURCELL is best known as the creator of *Sam and Max*, the dog and rabbit crime-fighting duo who debuted in comic-book form in 1987, and went on to appear in a video game and an animated TV series. Steve has worked with LucasArts on video games including *Indiana Jones, The Dig, the Monkey Island series,* and *Sam and Max Hit the Road*, and currently works at Pixar.

PHILIP CRAIG RUSSELL, a graduate of the University of Cincinnati with a degree in painting, has run the gamut in comics. After establishing a name for himself at Marvel, he went on to become one of the pioneers in opening new vistas for this underestimated field. His award-winning opera adaptations includ[redacted]ive-hundred page, two-volume *Ring of the Nibelung* from Dark Horse, [redacted] many others, including *The Magic Flute*, currently being collected in a three-volume set from NBM, where he also continues his ongoing project retelling the fairy tales of Oscar Wilde. Russell has done several projects with Neil Gaiman, including *The Sandman* and *Murder Mysteries*, and along the way has become a highly respected artist's artist with his fine-lined, realistic style, and revolutionary storytelling.

JIM STA[redacted]LIN was born in Detroit, Michigan in 1949. He served in the U.S. Navy [redacted]968 to 1971, as a photographer's mate. In 1972, he started his comics ca[redacted]er at Marvel, and has been working on and off with comics ever since. Comics work includes *Breed, Captain Marvel, Cosmic Odyssey, Dreadstar, Master of Kung Fu, Thanos Quest, The End of the Marvel Universe,* and stints on almost every major character in mainstream comics.He co-wrote four novels with Diana Graziunas, and is the co-founder of Electric Prism, a software design and new-media company in Woodstock, New York.

DAVE STEVENS was born and raised in Portland, Oregon, but he still turned out okay. In the nearly thirty years since his big break inking the legendary Russ Manning on *Tarzan*, he has won extraordinary acclaim of his own for [redacted]ntings and illustrations. In 1991, Disney made his comic series *The Rock*[redacted]into a major motion picture.

CAMERON STEWART is one of four founding members of The Royal Academy of Illustration and Design, a comics collective in Toronto. He has drawn stories for Dark Horse in *B.P.R.D.: Soul of Venice* and *Tales of the Vamp*[redacted]tten by series creators Mike Mignola and Joss Whedon, respectively. He ha[redacted]ed extensively for DC Comics, including an acclaimed run on *Catwoman* with Ed Brubaker, and as artist and co-creator of *Seaguy* with Grant Morrison. He is indestructible when exposed to sunlight.

DAVE STEWART started out as a design intern at Dark Horse, and is now the award-winning colorist of *Hellboy* and many, many other books. In addition to coloring some of the best artists in comics, he practices kung fu, speaks

Cherokee, and raises chihuahuas, which makes him a cross-cultural triple threat in his native state of Idaho, and keeps him up most nights.

BEN TEMPLESMITH is a semi-living legend on the comic-book convention circuit. Contrary to popular mythology, Ben was not raised by dingoes and he doesn't drink *that* much tequila. He does, however, draw a great deal of comic books, which to-date include *Criminal Macabre, 30 Days of Night, Hellspawn, Singularity 7, Dark Days,* and *Return to Barrow.*

CRAIG THOMPSON was born in Traverse City, Michigan in 1975 and raised outside a small town in central Wisconsin. His first graphic novel *Good-Bye, Chunky Rice,* won him the 1999 Harvey Award for Best New Talent along with nominations for Eisner, Ignatz, Firecracker, and Eagle awards. While working on his second graphic novel, *Blankets,* Craig paid the bills writing, drawing, and designing comics and illustrations for Dark Horse, Nickelodeon, DC Comics, Marvel, OWL, National Geographic Kids, and a myriad of other publications. He currently resides in Portland, Oregon.

JILL THOMPSON is a renowned illustrator and the creator of the award-winning, all-ages cartoon book series *Scary Godmother.* Her work has been seen in books ranging from *Classics Illustrated* and *Wonder Woman* to *Sandman.* Jill is a longtime resident of Chicago, where she lives with her husband, comic-book writer Brian Azzarello.

Before going freelance, KEVIN WALKER designed confectionery packaging for people with no imagination. His career in comics began with England's *2000 AD,* and was interrupted by a stint as Concept Artist on the *Judge Dredd* film. Other credits include designs for Game Workshops, cards for *Magic the Gathering,* several computer games, and comics written and illustrated for DC Comics, Dark Horse, and Marvel. He lives and works in Yorkshire, England, where he struggles with his first novel and the fading dreams of becoming the British Olympic sprint champion.

After receiving an MFA in Printmaking from Penn State, SIMEON WILKINS thought Hollywood the next logical step. He met Guillermo del Toro while slinging DVDs to celebrities in Los Angeles, and got his first big break storyboarding the *Hellboy* movie. Now busy boarding a CG feature for Sony Pictures, Simeon still finds time to work on comics and teach his ten-month-old son, Evan, all about giant monster movies.

J.H. WILLIAMS III is an Eisner Award-winning artist who has worked in the comics industry since 1991. He has done projects for DC, Marvel, Dark Horse, and Humanoids, among others, but his most noted work thus far is *Promethea,* co-created with Alan Moore, for Wildstorm. J.H. currently resides in California's central valley with his wife and business manager Wendy who tolerates his toy/music/comic/monster movie/Adriana Lima and Bettie Page obsessions.

AKIRA YOSHIDA has been writing and creating in the Japanese manga and anime industries for years. A long-time fan of American comic books, he prayed for the day when he would be able to break down international borders and write in the United States. With this *Hellboy* story, he sees that wish fulfilled. He credits the anime *Akira* for his success as it is the only reason American editors can remember his name.

HELLBOY

by MIKE MIGNOLA

SEED OF DESTRUCTION
with John Byrne
ISBN: 1-59307-094-2 $17.95

WAKE THE DEVIL
ISBN: 1-59307-095-0 $17.95

**THE CHAINED COFFIN
AND OTHERS**
ISBN: 1-59307-091-8 $17.95

THE RIGHT HAND OF DOOM
ISBN: 1-59307-093-4 $17.95

CONQUEROR WORM
ISBN: 1-59307-092-6 $17.95

THE ART OF HELLBOY
ISBN: 1-59307-089-6 $29.95

HELLBOY WEIRD TALES
Volume 1
By John Cassaday, Jason Pearson,
Eric Powell, Alex Maleev,
Bob Fingerman and others
ISBN: 1-56971-622-6 $17.95

HELLBOY WEIRD TALES
Volume 2
By John Cassaday, JH Williams III,
P. Craig Russell, Jim Starlin,
Frank Cho, Evan Dorkin and others
ISBN: 1-56971-953-5 $17.95

**B.P.R.D. HOLLOW EARTH
AND OTHERS**
By Mike Mignola, Chris Golden,
Ryan Sook and others
ISBN: 1-56971-862-8 $17.95

**B.P.R.D. THE SOUL OF VENICE
AND OTHERS**
By Mike Oeming, Guy Davis,
Scott Kolins, Geoff Johns and others
ISBN: 1-59307-132-9 $17.95

ODD JOBS
Short stories by Mike Mignola,
Poppy Z. Brite, Chris Golden and others
Illustrations by Mike Mignola
ISBN: 1-56971-440-1 $14.95

ODDER JOBS
Short stories by Frank Darabont,
Guillermo del Toro and others
Illustrations by Mike Mignola
ISBN: 1-59307-226-0 $14.95

HELLBOY BASEBALL CAP
#17-106 $14.95

**HELLBOY LUNCHBOX
(& POSTCARD) 2**
Tin de-bossed full color
#11-836 $19.99

HELLBOY PVC SET
#10-666 $39.99

HELLBOY JOURNAL
#12-309 $9.99

HELLBOY TALKING BOARD
Pressed paper playing board with
wooden planchette
#10-248 $24.99

HELLBOY ZIPPO LIGHTER
#17-101 $29.95

DARK HORSE COMICS™ *drawing on your nightmares*
darkhorse.com